It's a Battle

Sidney Langford

Companion Press
P.O. Box 310
Shippensburg, PA 17257

"Good Stewards of the
Manifold Grace of God"

ISBN 1-56043-625-5

For Worldwide Distribution
Printed in the U.S.A.

Dedicated
to
My Darling Wife Jennie

Acknowledgments

The challenge to write this book is the result of the prayers and encouragement of many friends. Following numerous speaking engagements, there were those who said, "You ought to write a book." The multiplicity of such remarks sparked the idea, "Well, maybe I should." I thought perhaps it would be good to record something for the family, but after I started, my real motivation was to tell of the thrilling and great things the Lord has done.

Down through the years God gave me a burden for the needs of the whitened harvest field, to reach the un-reached in the regions beyond, and to strive to complete the unfinished task. The measure, in which we have been able to accomplish this, is a result of the warm-hearted, cooperative team effort of our fellow-missionaries and a faithful constituency in the homeland who have upheld us in fervent prayer. This has also been very evident in the publishing of this book. My wife Jennie and our children, Lois, David, Ginny and Ron, and their families cheered me on. My wife worked laboriously at the computer and Ginny's artistic ability produced the cover. Stalwart friends (some accomplished writers and secretarial experts)—Willis Snow, Marge White, and my sister, Virginia Fletcher—scrutinized the contents meticulously and made excellent suggestions. Missionary colleagues—William Beatty, Barbara Battye, Martha Hughell and others—were consulted, and they reviewed the parts they were familiar with.

As we send forth the book, *It's a Battle*, it is with the prayer that the Lord will use it to stir hearts to action on behalf of missionaries, the national church and its leadership who are in the midst of the conflict, and the millions who are still outside the fold of Christ.

To each one who has had a part, I say, "Thank you."

Sidney Langford

Endorsements

"Sid and Jennie Langford have chronicled the faithfulness of the unchanging Lord Jesus Christ throughout their entire life and ministry with Africa Inland Mission. Their moving accounts of God's evident love, mercy, and power in the face of danger and hardship is a compelling inspiration in God's hands to challenge one to the total joy of abandonment to God's good and perfect will."

> Ted Barnett, U.S. Director
> Africa Inland Mission International
> Pearl River, NY

"It has often been debated whether people make the times, or the times make the people. Sidney Langford's book, *It's a Battle*, reminds us that it is God who makes both the people and the times.

"This is the thrilling story of dedicated men and women, real people, serving the Lord Jesus Christ in Africa in the most turbulent of times at great personal sacrifice. They would not call it sacrifice. For them, such years of commitment and challenge were God's will in which they gladly rejoiced.

"This chronicle of missions will bless you abundantly...and will deepen your personal faith in the Lord Jesus. I'm glad I read this book. You'll be glad when you read it, too."

Donald R. Hubbard
Former pastor, Calvary Baptist Church,
New York City
Former pastor, Bibletown Community Church
Boca Raton, FL

"In 14 brief, but well-written chapters, Sidney Langford gives us the story of his conversion and call to the mission field, along with the challenge he faced as a missionary in Zaire and Sudan, and as U.S. Director of the Africa Inland Mission. Interwoven throughout these pages is the sweeping history of the A.I.M.—from its early beginnings almost a century ago to the present hour.

"To read this book is to feel the pulse and heartbeat of modern-day missions. Sidney Langford has ably captured in words the trials and triumphs of missionary life, and powerfully relates what God has done—and will do—through those who are prepared to be 'claim stakers' in reaching a spiritually dark world for Christ. This is recommended reading for all who aspire to serve the Lord in the cause of missions.

Stephen F. Olford
President of Encounter Ministries, Inc.
Stephen Olford Center for Biblical
Preaching
Memphis, TN

"This is a heart-warming and encouraging record of the faithfulness of our Lord. The history is informative and beautifully illustrated. The power of the Lord is clear, and the response to the call of God is heart-warming. The Langfords represent all that is noble and uplifting in missionary response and service. Biblical missions is faithfully presented and relevantly seen in action. If you want to see pioneer endeavor and tremendous progress over challenging obstacles, this is the book for you!"

> Paul E. Toms
> Dean of the Chapel,
> Gordon-Conwell Theological Seminary,
> South Hamilton, MA
> Pastor Emeritus Park Street Church
> Boston, MA

"*It's a Battle* tells of:

Courage in the face of danger. Humor, excitement, and romance all are a part of this life story of two veteran missionaries, depicting missionary life in Africa. This inspiring account reveals their deep moment-by-moment faith and trust in God, their obedience and their dependence upon Him. It is an exciting demonstration of the faithfulness of God, and it extends a challenge to the child of God."

> Marge White, Secretary to Senior Pastor,
> Hawthorne Gospel Church
> Hawthorne, NJ
> also served as Secretary on
> Missionary Conference Committee

"but the people that do know their God shall be strong, and do exploits" (Daniel 11:32b).

"For over 50 years Sid Langford has been one of my heroes. He is a missionary statesman whom I have come to love and respect.

"This book is a reminder that the Christian life is not a playground, but a battlefield. We need to join the army."

Jack Wyrtzen, Founder/Director
Word of Life International

Contents

Foreword

For nearly two thousand years the world has witnessed millions of persons who have believed in the life, death, and resurrection of Jesus Christ and have experienced the Christian's new birth. That identification has cost the lives of some Christians such as Stephen, David Livingstone, and Peter Cameron Scott. Others however, did not die, but demonstrated an unusual boldness for Christ as pioneer missionaries in distant lands. Although they faced the reality of taunts, testings, and temptations, they always came out victorious for the cause of Jesus Christ.

This latter group of Christians is characterized by Sidney and Jennie Langford. For nearly 60 years the Langfords have faced the challenges of frontier missions work in Africa and also as the U.S. Director of the Africa Inland Mission.

It's a Battle is a twentieth century chapter of God's chronology as He continues to build His Church on planet earth. The Holy Spirit-given optimism empowered the Langfords to accept countless challenges to overcome obstacles that appeared to be insurmountable, and to drive toward reaching as many people for Christ as possible. This book is the emblazoned story of the work of Jesus Christ through His servants, the Langfords.

It has been a privilege to read the manuscript about my friend Sid Langford, a 1933 PCB alumnus, and his dear wife Jennie. I commend the book to the reader, with the prayer that the Lord will give you a ready mind and heart to comprehend the burdened heart the author has for the mission of sharing Jesus Christ with the people of the world.

W. Sherrill Babb
President, Philadelphia College of Bible

Africa Inland Mission

Chapter 1

The Sleeping Giant

In ages past the continent of Africa was shrouded in mystery and spoken of as the Dark Continent or the Sleeping Giant. It was a challenge to the early explorers who penetrated the interior, seeking to unlock its mysteries and obtain its riches. They found it a land of contrasts with boundless deserts, mammoth forests of giant mahogany trees, towering mountains that spiraled up into the heavens, and ancient rivers flowing from its center in every direction toward the surrounding oceans. God's marvelous creation was inhabited not only by man, but also by a great variety of exotic birds and myriads of animals. They all displayed the beauty of His endowed handiwork.

Missionaries such as Robert Moffatt, David Livingstone, Henry Stanley, Alexander Mackay, and Mary Slessor followed hard in the footsteps of the explorers, seeking to penetrate the spiritual darkness with the Gospel of Light. They enjoyed the beauty of the land but also endured the hardships of heat, health hazards, and hostile tribes. They did this for one purpose, namely, to "hold forth the Word of Life" to the multitudes of people who were spiritually blind. The streams of "Living Water" spread far and wide in this spiritual desert and brought forth fruit in abundance.

European governments saw the great potential for expanding their borders on the continent and thus began the process of staking their claims, but not without resistance from indignant tribes. Strife gradually gave way to colonization. In some areas the people and land were exploited to a great extent, but the exploiters did bring about cessation of tribal wars and also provided schools and medical care to enhance the lives of the populace. In many countries, nationals climbed the educational and social ladders and were eventually able to meet the European at any level. They proved themselves able administrators and were given responsible positions. Unfortunately, this was not true in all the colonies. Some governments were fearful that this would stimulate a desire for independence.

In 1955 the Organization of African Unity held its first conference in Accra, Nigeria, and echoed the feelings that had been suppressed for years; namely, a desire for freedom from the yoke of colonialism. Tom Mboya, one of the keynote speakers, summed up his message and the feelings of most who attended with the words, "Scram, white man, scram!" Soon voices were heard from all corners of Africa. It was at this time that the Prime Minister of Great Britain, Mr. MacMillan, visited all their African colonies and reported to Parliament and the world, "A wind of change is blowing over Africa," and he urged that the British "Ship of State" adjust its sails.

As a result, other governments prepared to set their houses in order and moved toward independence with a measure of dignity. But there were some who sought to delay the day of reckoning and then were forced to make hasty preparations for the inevitable transfer of power. Because the Africans lacked trained leadership, an effort was made to give "crash courses," but without any experience this proved to be devastating and destructive. Some of the countries that demanded immediate independence were faced with unstable and volatile situations for years.

Although missions were not involved in the politics of these countries, they were sometimes accused by political aspirants of being linked with the colonizers. The national evangelical Christians and many of the general populace were not vindictive because they were well aware of the role the missionaries played in their countries. They lived among them and served them at the grass-roots level. The missionaries started schools, established clinics and hospitals, and ministered to them in love. This was for the purpose of making the gospel known.

Belgian Congo (now known as Zaire) is an example of what took place. It is a massive country in the very heart of Central Africa with its Mountains of the Moon, rolling hills and plains providing lush farmland, the great Ituri rain forest, and the mighty Congo River. Scattered throughout this beautiful area were two hundred tribes (consisting of twenty-five million people) who were caught in the vortex of political change. The

Congolese were not prepared for independence when, in 1960, power was hastily dropped into their laps, and the result was chaotic. Unruly drunken soldiers foraged without any control and took unreasonable vengeance on many of the Belgian people. A few missionaries were caught in the crossfire of this conflict, but for the most part they were able to carry on their ministries. The country was under considerable stress, and this was the seedbed for what grew into the politically motivated Simba (lions) rebellion, led by the followers of the first president, Lumumba, who had been assassinated. These, together with Congolese malcontents, were trained by foreign communistic elements established in Rwanda for the purpose of taking possession of the mineral rich northeast corner of the Congo.

Rebel soldiers.

I was in Zaire in the month of July, 1964. As we visited our various stations we came upon large groups of young men in remote areas, training for Simba subversive activity. As we traveled the roads, we could feel the spirit of antagonism and rebellion in the air, but little did our missionaries anticipate what would take place in Stanleyville just two weeks after I left Zaire and returned to the United States. We were shocked by the overthrow of the government in Stanleyville and by the manner in which the movement spread so rapidly throughout all northeastern Congo.

There seemed to be no resistance by local government officials. Many, together with leaders in the various communities, were slain immediately. Government buildings and banks were destroyed and the valuable records of the past were cast to the four winds. Missionaries and mission stations were not exempt from the carnage. During the year that followed, the lives of over 40 missionaries, together with some of their children, and thousands of African Christians were snuffed out. In the providence of God, all of our mission family was saved; some by the "skin of their teeth." They were spared in miraculous ways.

This was a crisis situation, and our mission family was in grave danger. Concerned for each member and also for their loved ones in the homeland, we endeavored to make contact with our missionaries in Congo by the way of "ham" radio. We needed to learn what was taking place. In the providence of God, the Lord provided us with an amateur radio operator, Mike Prall, who worked the airwaves tirelessly, maintaining a regular schedule with our Congo missionary, Ed Schuit, who did a masterful job of keeping us informed. At one point, gravely concerned about the safety of our missionaries who were endeavoring to evacuate, we decided to "go on the air" even though we did not have a schedule. You can imagine the thrill that was ours when we heard the voice of Myron Schuit, Ed's brother, saying, "This is a shot in the dark." He was trying to contact us with a final message before the last of our 145 missionaries left the Congo.

We were conscious of God's special undertaking as each of our missionary families crossed the border into friendly surrounding countries. Thrilling stories of the protecting hand of the Lord could be told by many of our missionaries. Some, whose furloughs were due, went on to the homeland, and others entered into various phases of work in other A.I.M. fields. Two of our missionaries, Chuck and Muriel Davis, were caught in the terrible holocaust of Stanleyville, but in the mercy of the Lord, their lives were spared. (This is recounted in the book, *Congo Crisis*, by Joseph T. Bayly.)

During the one-year absence of our mission family, the Church of Christ in Congo went through a terrible bloodbath. The Simbas pursued them in the forest and bushland day in and day out. Some fled with only their Bibles. It was a time of heart-searching and calling on the Lord. Some of our leaders who were being sought said, "We didn't pray; we just talked to the Lord." Such was their intimacy and dependence upon Him. There were those who were slain bearing a radiant testimony, and others were miraculously spared. Volumes could be written concerning this episode of the history of the Congo Church.

November 24, 1964, was the beginning of the reversal of the tide in the conflict. Belgian paratroopers were dropped on the city of Stanleyville to rescue 236 hostages held in the Victoria Hotel. Following this, central government forces led by mercenaries gradually began to recapture some of the key towns throughout the northeast. Such areas became military garrisons and havens of protection for those in the immediate locality. This forced the Simbas into the forest and bushland. From there they carried out night raids on villages, stealing food and cattle and burning down homes.

In the summer of 1965, plans were made for me to visit our fields in Africa. Before leaving, I obtained permission from the U.S. State Department to travel in Congo if the way should open for me to do so. The Simba conflict was still going on and none of our missionaries had been able to return. I was advised to stay in towns that had been recaptured by the government forces, which had established a military presence.

While still in the States I felt constrained to make a plane booking to fly from Nairobi, Kenya, to Leopoldville and from there to Stanleyville and on to Bunia in the northeast, which was located in the center of our Congo work. While traveling in Kenya I had hoped the Missionary Aviation Fellowship (MAF) would be able to obtain permission from the Congo government for me to fly from Nairobi to Bunia with Norman Weiss, who was the exiled Acting Congo Field Director. This would have been only a three-hour trip; however, because of the Simba conflict, permission was not granted. Then we made arrangements to fly on Air Congo from Nairobi to Leopoldville with the hope that we would be able to travel the same airline to

Bunia. In the meantime MAF would continue to try to obtain permission for a flight into Congo.

Norman Weiss and I arrived in Leopoldville on Tuesday afternoon and learned that before we could fly on to Bunia it would be necessary, because of military activity in the area, to obtain permission from three government offices. The missionaries living there questioned whether we could get these permits in one day (on Wednesday). The plane for Bunia would be leaving at 5:30 a.m. on Thursday. We realized that it would be nearly an impossible task and, therefore, made it a matter of earnest prayer.

Wednesday morning found us starting on our quest as early as possible. John Strash of the MAF, who knew his way around the city, kindly agreed to take us to the various offices. First we had to obtain a permit from the Minister of the Interior before applying for the others. When we arrived at the office, there was already a large crowd of 50 or more, and the group grew as we awaited the arrival of the Minister. After about an hour, an announcement was made that the Minister of the Interior would not be in that day, and everyone was dismissed. The three of us were a bit dumbfounded, but we decided to wait and make further inquiries as to whether the permit might be given by someone else. In answer to our question, we were either given a negative answer or told they didn't know. We continued to stand around, and of course, breathed up prayers for the Lord's special undertaking. He can make a way when there is no way.

Finally, after exhausting all our efforts, another Congolese gentleman, dressed in a business suit, came into the office, and we immediately approached him with the same question. He was very kind and sought to be helpful. He suggested going to another floor in the same building and to a certain room number. We did this hastily since precious time was passing. When we arrived at the closed door, we knocked and prayed at the same time. A voice from within told us to enter. As we did, we saw a Belgian official sitting behind a desk. He was the Assistant to the Congolese Minister of the Interior, and within a few minutes Norman and I had the first important permit.

We rushed off to another section of the city to the office of the "Surete" to see the top official of the country's security police. A white-haired Congolese official greeted us warmly and, after making sure we had the Minister's signature, quickly stamped the Seal of the Surete and scribbled his signature. We were mindful of the fact that if the Minister of the Interior had been in, no doubt all that large crowd, which had been dismissed from his office, would have been at this office ahead of us. As it were there was no one else on hand.

It was now "two signatures down" and one to go. We kept our eyes on our watches. It was past noon and many of the government offices close around 2 p.m., so off we went. It was good that John knew his way to the other end of the city, to the "Bureau de Militaire." Since we were going into a military zone, their sanction had to be granted. When we got there our hearts sank; we saw about two hundred others waiting to get similar permission. We quickly got into the line. We couldn't help wondering, "will we even get our passports handed in, or if we do, will we get them back or be told to come back tomorrow?" To our great joy and surprise, our names were called out to pick up our passports, signed and sealed. They were all obtained in a miraculous one-day period of time! The Lord had gone before; He made a way through the wilderness of "red tape"!

At three o'clock on Thursday morning, Norman and I made our way to the airport. The booking I had made in the United States before leaving had been confirmed. Norman had made booking on the same plane but could only be wait-listed. When we arrived at the airport, there must have been three or four hundred Congolese on hand clamoring to get up to the weighing-in desks. With baggage in hand, and with great difficulty, I finally got the formalities cared for and my baggage tagged for boarding. Then I was hurried off into another section of the airport and separated from Norman. I anxiously waited for him, hoping he would get on.

Time passed, and he still had not arrived. I was shuttled on toward the boarding area. The four-motored plane looked pretty much the worse for wear, and every seat was taken. Norman had not been able to get on. Only a few other white folks were on board. We were soon off, climbing into the sky as the morning sun arose. The drone of the motors was monotonous. About three hours later we were circling over Stanleyville.

I thought of the Belgian airdrop over that city a few months before. At that time Dr. Paul Carlson and a number of others had lost their lives. We were told that Simbas were still hiding in the massive forest area around Stanleyville and that they took pot shots at the planes as they came in. However, we arrived without incident.

As we disembarked on the airstrip, we could see a number of war planes on the ground. Some had the head of a buffalo painted on the nose of the aircraft with the word "Makasi" (strong-strength) painted in large letters beneath it. We waited in a crowded, warm room. We learned that sometimes the Air-Congo plane got this far, then the military commandeered the gasoline. They would then have to terminate the trip at this point, so we were apprehensive.

After about an hour, we were called for boarding and soon were soaring over the seemingly endless green jungle of the Ituri forest. Again I thought of the Unevangelized Fields Mission missionaries, Al Larson, and our own Chuck and Muriel Davis, who had gone through such an ordeal during the Stanleyville holocaust, and of some of the faithful servants who were buried in the forest below. About two and a half hours later we landed at the Bunia airport. A large group of people was on hand, no doubt hoping to possibly meet some relative or to catch up on news of what was happening elsewhere.

No one knew I was coming in on the plane. There was no means of communication to inform church leaders, and I didn't even know who was there. The revolution had scattered everyone. They told us that the plane we had traveled on would not be carrying any passengers on its return because it was not considered safe! It was good to be back in Bunia again. Just a short time before, this small town of about 35 thousand had been recaptured from the Simbas by the Congo government forces.

It was necessary for us to go through immigration formalities. As I stood there in the small airport building, I prayed for the Lord to lead in accordance with His plan. I didn't know anyone there. Then suddenly a

Congolese man came up to me, spoke to me in Bangala, and shook my hand warmly. He said I had baptized him at Aba station some years before. Happy to see me, he went off to call one of the local officials who had returned with the army. He was one of our Bunia Christians. He too, was very exuberant in his welcome.

Word of my arrival spread and brought Fanwele Pasha, a fine church leader, to the airport. He flung his arms around me and immediately arranged with the official to take me in a vehicle recaptured from the Simbas. It was a very beat-up conveyance, and the door had to be tied shut. Off we went to the town which was about a mile away. It showed evidence of the ravages of war. Shop windows were smashed and buildings pockmarked by bullet holes. Nearly all the buildings had been broken into, ransacked, or destroyed. I wondered what condition I would find the Mission home in. It had been the residence and office of the Congo Field Director. When we arrived I was amazed to find everything intact and only two bullet holes in the roof. Two of the African men who had worked there were on hand and they took good care of me. They prepared food and did other household chores. They all gave me a hearty welcome. This was to be my base of operation for the next 11 days.

None of our A.I.M. missionaries were in Congo at the time. A few Greek merchants had recently returned to ascertain their losses. Bill Deans, of the Christian Mission to Many Lands, had come back a short time before and was at their mission station at Nyankunde, about 25 miles away.

The commanding officer of the Central Government forces (a national) was very kind to me. He provided a jeep and two soldiers to accompany me on a trip to Bogoro station to make a contact with the church leaders and infirmiers (male nurses). This was the first trip I made outside of the Bunia area, and I was a bit apprehensive, not knowing if Simba rebels were still hiding in that locality. The contact I had with our pastors and Christians at Bogoro was heart-warming. All the missionaries' homes had been pilfered, but the dispensary nursing personnel functioned as well as they possibly could with their limited medical supplies.

When the news of my arrival in Bunia spread, numerous visitors came to see me. Many told stories of miraculous deliverance from Simba atrocities. Others, however, paid dearly with their lives, and their testimonies continue to live on.

I made contact with Bill Deans, a stalwart leader of the Brethren work for more than 45 years and a warm colleague in the work of the Lord. Bill's car had been retrieved from the Simbas by the Congo forces, and he made it available to me to travel to other A.I.M. stations. Fanwele Pasha accompanied me. Blukwa station was about 60 miles up in the hills amidst the lush green vegetation of the area.

Upon our arrival we were given a royal welcome by the pastor and the teacher of the secondary school. All seven of the missionary homes had been looted. During the Simba rule, the pastor had narrowly escaped with his life; and there he was to tell of God's marvelous intervention. He told us that as the Simbas banged on the front door of his home one night, he escaped by the back door and fled for the bush. The most thrilling part of the welcome was when about 20 or more orphan children jubilantly sang hymns and danced around me. They, together with the girls in the large girls' work, had been nurtured and supervised by Olive Love. Fanwele and I spent the night at Blukwa. In view of all I heard about the Simbas, one could not help wondering if some were lurking in the shadows.

The next day we went on to Linga station where we have a Bible School. Many of the students had scattered as a result of the rebellion. However, we were thrilled to see the few who had returned, cutting the grass and cleaning up the station after the ravages of the Simba onslaught. All four houses had been robbed of their contents. I remembered such warm fellowship with those who had labored there: Ed and Nellie Schuit, Myron and Beatrice Schuit, John and Dorothy Gration, and Jack Litchman. The evidence of their faithful ministry remained. The students eagerly asked all sorts of questions, especially concerning the return of their missionaries. I encouraged them to pray and prepare for their return.

I then went on to the lovely station of Rethy located in the hills at a 7,000-foot altitude. This was a central station with Rethy Academy for MK's (missionary kids). It had classrooms and dormitories for about 70 children in addition to teachers' homes. The printing press and bookshop were there, as well as the oculist department and the large hospital. My memory took me back to the days when our four children had attended the academy. It was a station with much activity and a vibrant church. Now the homes were left desolate, the classrooms strewn with papers and books, the dormitories devastated, and the lovely pianos smashed to bits. The press building and equipment were all intact because the Simbas had been persuaded to preserve them for their use. We found the hospital functioning but with very little medication, which had been hidden from the Simbas. The buildings were intact because the Simbas thought they might need them. I was given a hearty welcome, especially by several hundred Congo school children. Their teacher had regathered them after the Simbas had been forced to flee from the government troops. The children were jubilant, and this was one of my rewards for coming.

The hour was getting a bit late, and I had planned to get back to Blukwa that night. However, an African pastor from Kasengu station was recuperating at the hospital and he persuaded me to go to Kasengu. It was with a measure of hesitancy I decided to go because of the possibility of being attacked by some Simbas. It was 17 miles across the hilly terrain. I learned that our car was the first to ride over that road since the rebels had left. The burnt-down houses of nearly all the Alur tribe in that area blazed the rebel trail. The Alur tribe children had been brainwashed by the Lumumba rebels. They led the Simbas to their parents' homes where they slew some and stole their cattle. A large Roman Catholic Church was left in a heap of ashes.

Some of the village people had returned and were in the process of rebuilding. What joy it was to meet the pastor and his wife. They were thrilled to see me. The Simbas had burnt down one of the missionary's homes and a number of African houses, but the large clinic, the school classrooms, and the church were all intact. I heard the sad story of the death of some who had been slain in the conflict. I also learned of a special evangelistic effort that had been carried on down near Lake Albert (Mobutu), right under the noses of the Simbas. I sought to encourage the church leaders and infirmiers and told them that, with the help of the Lord, missionaries would be returning. After prayer, committing them to the Lord, I bade them farewell. During the night hours I arrived back at Blukwa and the next morning I went on to Bunia, with a heart filled with praise for the Lord's undertaking.

Bill Deans and I talked about the possibility of making a trip by car together to Oicha station, which was in the heart of the Ituri forest. We learned that Simbas

Barrier guarded by government soldiers.

were secluded in their forest hideouts during the daylight hours and at night they raided the African villages along the main road. The villagers, of course, would flee and their grain would be stolen. Sometimes their houses were burnt to the ground. We were given a military escort for the trip: one Congolese soldier with his rifle! He was really our "password" through all the military roadblocks, and this saved hours of time.

Ready for action.

As we went through the winding forest road with the tall, gigantic mahogany trees on either side, we were apprehensive as to what we might find around each curve. With gratitude to the Lord we arrived in the small town of Beni, about one hundred miles in the forest. This was also a military base for government soldiers. This was where we were to spend the night with the lone Greek merchant who was protected by the military. He took good care of us.

The next morning Bill and I drove out to Oicha station about eight miles on the forest road. This was a large medical station that had been started back in the early 1930's by Dr. Carl K. Becker, and the work had "grown like Topsy" as buildings were added to meet the ever-expanding needs. Nearly one thousand patients had been cared for daily, and a leprosarium held several thousand patients. Dr. and Mrs. Becker and their staff had been harrassed on several occasions by rowdy drunken soldiers and those who were politically motivated, seeking to exert a show of power. The Oicha missionaries remained adamant and carried on their work.

However, in 1964 the attacks became more violent. The Simba revolutionary movement was communistically inspired, desirous of attaining the goals of their first president, Lumumba, who had been slain. The rebels had determined to take Oicha, and it was only when the murderous hordes got dangerously close and the outcome seemed inevitable, that the Beckers and their staff of 190 nationals and missionaries reluctantly but miraculously crossed over into Uganda without the loss of any lives. In the providence of God, they were given permission by the Ugandan Government to open a hospital that had been closed at Nyabarongo, and in a few weeks' time were ministering to nearly seven hundred patients daily.

Now more than a year had passed, and the Congolese government forces had been able to recapture the area around the towns of Beni and Oicha. When Bill Deans and I arrived at Oicha, we were given a hearty welcome by the people and some of the infirmiers who had returned. I quickly made a survey of the damage done in each of the ravaged missionary homes. The rebels had tried to burn down the home of Dr. Becker by starting a fire in the bathroom. The room was charred black, but fortunately the fire did not get through the mud plaster on the walls. The hospital was still intact, and patients were already coming to be cared for. We were mindful of the fact that we would soon have to return to Nyankunde and would have to get through the thick forest area while we still had daylight. We did this without incident or car breakdown, and we gave praise to God. It was dark when we arrived at Nyankunde station.

The day following our return to Nyankunde I was booked to return to Leopoldville on Air Congo. I had been in Congo for eight days, and I was reluctant to leave. I felt my job was not yet completed. I had hoped to get to Aba station where we had first served and to other stations. With a heavy heart I drove to Bunia airport in the afternoon, accompanied by Bill Deans, Fanwele Pasha, and other church leaders. The small airport was crowded with waiting passengers and some mercenaries. We waited for several hours past the time the plane was due to arrive. Finally an announcement was made that the plane had not been able to depart from Stanleyville because the military had commandeered all the fuel. The next plane was expected a week later. (Actually, it arrived one month later.)

With joy I was taken back to our Bunia base. I didn't know what I would be doing, but I committed the matter to the Lord. One hour after I returned to the Bunia home, I heard a small plane, which went on to land at the airport. Could this by any chance be the MAF? Had they finally received permission to land in Bunia? Since Bill had returned to Nyankunde, I didn't have a car. So, Fanwele went by bike to ascertain if it was the MAF. Within a short time I learned that it was and that Les Brown, the pilot, had brought Dr. Becker and Bill Stough. What a meeting that was! Dr. Becker was soon whisked off to perform emergency surgery at Nyankunde Hospital.

With the MAF plane at our disposal, Bill Stough and I made plans to fly to Aba, Dungu, Watsa, and then return to Bunia. We hoped to do this in one day. It was about eight hundred miles by road and would take nearly a week, but all bushland areas were still infested with Simbas. Early the next morning, Les took off with three passengers, Bill and I and a brother of Chief Ali, who had miraculously escaped the hands of the Simbas. Bill had also served at Aba, and we were both looking forward to getting back into our "home" territory.

The mercenaries had captured Aba Poste from the Simbas a short time before, and they were based in the Poste area. As we got close to Aba there was quite a bit of cloud coverage. We could see some of the area through the breaking clouds. I knew approximately where the airstrip was because I had cleared it years before when the first MAF plane had made a survey in Congo. We flew in the general area, but couldn't locate it because of the clouds. Les was an excellent pilot and decided to try to go below the clouds. As we came through the cloud layer we were right over the Aba road and a truck on it loaded with Africans who were startled by the appearance of a plane. The truck stopped immediately, and all the Congolese occupants jumped off and scattered in the bush. They thought they were about to be attacked. As we circled below the clouds, we found the airfield and landed without incident. Soon mercenaries arrived with their commanding officer, and gave us a fine welcome. Aba township had been shot up as a result of the battle that had taken place, and a lot of captured war material was displayed.

We were taken to Aba Mission station about three miles away. Arriving on "hospital hill," Bill and I stepped out of the jeep. The African infirmiers who were on hand could hardly believe their eyes. They were stunned; how did we get there? Bill went down to see the condition of his home, and I started on a quick survey of the other dwellings. The hospital was intact, but the homes were wrecked inside. Going down one of the back paths, I met Arona Bakonzi, an evangelist, who had not heard of our arrival. He looked at me in amazement and with tears in his eyes, flung his arms about me and said, "Bwana, yo asirakumi!" "Bwana, you have come!" When I got down to where Bill was, there were groups of older African women who had known him from childhood. Each woman took her turn to hug him and affectionately welcome him home!

Because our time was limited, we had someone beat the station drum. Soon the comparatively few (about two hundred) who had returned from hiding in the bush showed up at the church. I spoke to them for about 15 minutes, telling them about their missionaries and that, with the help of the Lord, they would return. Our hearts were saddened to learn of the martyrdom of Pastor Yakobo Marako and others whose lives had been snuffed out as a result of the revolution. It made our hearts heavy to have to bid farewell to these dear people after such a hasty and meaningful visit. The captain of the mercenaries took us to the Aba airport.

Before we took off for Dungu 135 miles away, we were cautioned by the captain that the landing strip there had been mined by the Simbas and that we must be given clearance by the mercenaries to land. We flew over familiar territory and in 45 minutes were over the town of Dungu where the large rivers of Uwele and Dungu meet together. Near their junction is a large castle that had been built by a Belgian administrator. The mercenaries were living there. We parachuted a note to them, asking if it was safe for us to land. The signal of a sheet, waved from the top of the castle, affirmed that we could land.

The airstrip is close to the Dungu Mission station. Within a few minutes we were rolling to a stop, there to be confronted by a jeep full of mercenaries out to greet us and find out who we were. We learned from them that just two days before, the last of 90 land mines had been removed from the strip. We knew the Lord had gone before. In a matter of minutes, Pastor Barnaba Boimatoni jubilantly came to welcome us. The last news we had heard of him was that he had been murdered by the Simbas, and lo and behold, here he was alive!

What a thrill it was to gather with him and about ten others on the hilltop where the mission was located. They told us how the Simbas had hotly pursued Joan Utting and Ray and Alice Faulkner, missionaries who fled for safety to the Sudan border. These missionaries were unaware that they had been pursued. The Lord had miraculously preserved His servants. This was a cause for praise. The little group stood around and listened as we told them of the purpose of our trip—to strengthen their hands in the hands of God and to assure them that with the help of the Lord, their missionaries would return. We had a time of prayer together, then we were off to the plane and on our way.

Our destination was the mining town of Watsa, nestled in the rolling hill country 110 miles away. It was raining lightly as we buzzed the military camp and then headed for the airfield on the other side of the town. We were met by an army officer, who drove us through the bullet-scarred town to the small compact mission compound and bookshop at one end of the main street. The rooms were practically empty except for a few metal bed frames, books on the floor, and a wrecked refrigerator. I listed the few remaining contents, and then on we went to see if we could find Pastor Yakobo at the Africa Inland Church compound. This was the plot of ground I had obtained from the former Paramount Chief Mangwanga 25 years before, and it was still a shining gospel beacon over the town.

The road was washed out so we had to walk up the hill. Pastor Yakobo was digging a small garden near his home, his back toward us as we approached quietly. When he turned to see who was coming, he could not believe it was Bill and I. Tears filled his eyes as he greeted us with real emotion. He and his family had been spared in the midst of the Simba onslaught, but we learned of others whose lives were taken in cold blood. We had prayer together and then reluctantly had to bid him farewell. The daylight hours were fast drawing to a close. We took off and headed for Bunia. We arrived just at dusk in the midst of a thunderstorm and torrential rain that made it difficult to get onto the airfield.

We had traveled 457 miles that day, flown for four hours (it would have taken five days to do this by road), visited three mission stations, listed the contents and conditions of all the mission property, and heard marvelous stories of deliverance. We had contacted hundreds of the Lord's people and left them with our hearts saddened and yet encouraged. We were conscious of the Lord's presence and His special undertaking each step of the way, and we were filled with praise and thanksgiving to God.

The next day, Saturday, Dr. Becker and Bill Deans joined us as we flew south to Oicha Medical Center. Instead of the eight-hour car trip that Bill Deans and I had taken the week before, we now flew over the Ituri forest and landed in 35 minutes at a large airstrip several miles from Oicha. A Greek merchant, who lived a few miles away in the small town of Beni, met us and drove us in his car to the hospital station. We went through numerous villages along the forest road, and the villagers were curious as to who was in the car. When some recognized Dr. Becker, the cry of excitement and amazement, "Mungunga Beka," was heard all along the way. Many came closer to get a better view as the car passed by. We all responded, exuberantly waving to them. Their jubilant cries followed us all the way to Oicha, and a huge crowd emerged from every area of the station. Their enthusiasm was so great that they pressed in around the good doctor; some wanted to put him up on their shoulders. Dr. Becker was overwhelmed by their welcome but he shied away from any such emotional display; instead he shook their hands enthusiastically.

Dr. Carl Becker's jubilant return to Oicha.

We made our way around the large hospital complex, which had been ravaged by the Simbas. When we came to the operating theaters, we could see that some activity was going on. A woman who had suffered from a strangulated hernia for the past four days was strapped to the operating table and would have died without the operation. The medical assistants who had worked with Dr. Becker had decided to try to save the woman's life but realized the procedure was probably beyond their ability. One can imagine their thrill when they saw the doctor's face. Within a short time he was scrubbed up and performing the surgery.

Dr. Becker spent a long session with members of the medical staff who had come back to the station, discussing the status of the equipment and what they had been able to salvage in the way of supplies. Then we were served a sumptuous feast of African food. At the end of a long tiring day, we went to the town of Beni and were shown warm hospitality by our Greek friend.

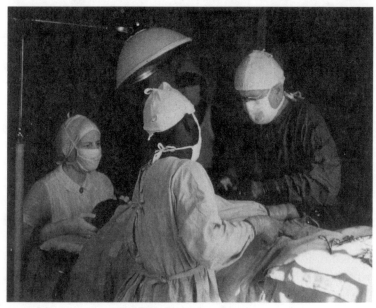

Dr. Becker in surgery.

Sunday was a "high day," a feast of good things. We all went back to Oicha for the Sunday morning service. The news of the doctor's arrival brought nearly everyone from the surrounding area. The large brick church was filled with more than a thousand people. Pastor Zephania Kasali led the service, and the church rang with hymns of praise to our wonderful Lord for His goodness and mercy in the midst of all the trials that had come their way. When Dr. Becker spoke, the crowd listened quietly as he told how the Lord had undertaken for him and all the staff who had gone to Uganda. Now they were ready to return. Zephania had asked me to bring the message, and what a thrill it was to speak on such an occasion, especially after all that had transpired during the past 11 days.

It was the beginning of the climax of our Congo trip, and the Lord had done the "exceeding abundantly above all that we could ask or think," (Eph. 3:20) not only for us but also for the Congo church. They had endured a "bloodbath" of persecution and, in spite of physical and material losses, had emerged triumphant. The church had been purged, purified, and strengthened in its commitment to the Lord. As I spoke, I was conscious of the Lord's presence and power; God worked in all our hearts. Following the service, the great crowd bade us farewell, then we were taken to the plane. In a short time Les Brown, our MAF pilot, was heading eastward toward Nairobi, Kenya. In the late afternoon a group of Congo missionaries greeted us at Wilson airport.

The next morning, Monday, the exiled Congo Field Council met together in Nairobi. As a result of the reports that were given, earnest prayer was made to the One who is able to "open a door that no man can shut" (see Rev. 3:8), seeking His leading with reference to the return of our Congo Mission family. The decision, made under the guidance of the Holy Spirit, was outlined with the steps to be taken. This was really the climax of our trip that had started 12 days before when we flew to Leopoldville (Kinshasa). A few days after this, Norman and Naomi Weiss led our first group of Congo missionaries back by road. At first there were only a few, but as others could be released from their Kenya assignments they returned to the land of their adoption. As we pondered all that the Lord had done in answer to prayer, we could say, "This is the Lord's doing; it is marvellous in our eyes" (Ps. 118:23).

Chapter 2

As It Was in the Beginning

...and John Thomas Langford begat Chris Langford in Barrow-in-Furness, Lancashire, England in 1889: In 1908 he left his father's household and went west to the New World, the land of the U.S.A., to the city of Philadelphia. Like Noah, he was a shipbuilder, both in England and in his new abode. His specialty was electrical engineering, which presented twentieth century opportunities. After two years of hard work, he anxiously awaited the arrival of his "bonnie" English lassie, Alice Muriel Burn, from Newcastle-on-Tyne, and they were married on the day of her arrival.

...and Chris and Alice begat Sidney on May 1, 1912. The process of adjusting to an American culture was slow for mother. Her strong "Jordie" Newcastle accent, English idioms and expressions were different from her neighbors. She became homesick and longed for the "old country" and friends. When I was six months old, the family returned to England. However, after a year and a half, we were back in Philadelphia again and Dad put down his roots.

Dad was a hard-working family man, pleasant and jovial, always seeking to make good provision for those of his household. Mother was all that one could wish for. She showered me with her love and concern even though, during the "terrible two's," I presented her with some anxious moments. The arrival of my sister, Virginia, brought new joy to our household. She was beautiful and chubby; Mom and Dad, when comparing her with their first-born, said she took the prize for being a good baby. No doubt it was difficult for me, a five-year-old who had previously enjoyed undivided parental attention, to have to share my parents with little "Ginny." However, brotherly love grew. On one occasion when baby sister took ill, unbeknown to others, I walked several city blocks to our family doctor's home and knocked on the door to inform him that Ginny was sick!

Early in Dad's life he had attended a Baptist Sunday School and church in Barrow-in-Furness, and so naturally he and Alice went to a Baptist church in Philadelphia at 28th & Lehigh Avenue. When the children came, we attended faithfully as a family. As a boy of six or seven, I well remember sitting under the preaching of Pastor Cope, a godly man, who fervently preached the whole counsel of God. He had an outgoing personality, showing the love of Christ and warning of the judgment to come.

The devastating flu epidemic of 1918, which took such a heavy toll upon the lives of the populace, also invaded our little household. Fortunately, it did not affect Mother and she worked around the clock, endeavoring to care for each of us. Dad was hit hard and became delirious. We feared that he would succumb to the plague. Our family physician, Dr. Allen, was actually a part of the family. He worked feverishly and Mother carried out all his instructions, until gradually the crisis passed.

During that time Pastor Cope felt constrained to urge Dad to accept Christ as his Savior and make an open profession of faith. Dad responded affirmatively, but said he felt like a coward doing this on what might be his deathbed. He promised Pastor Cope that he would take the stand the first Sunday he could get to church. He kept his word. Evidently, Mother had accepted Christ while in England and she always gave evidence of her desire to follow the Lord. Although the family moved on several occasions, we always found our way to a Baptist church.

Mother and Dad and sister Virginia.

On the first Sunday in our new abode in Fox Chase, Philadelphia, I attended Bethany Baptist Sunday School, and my parents became affiliated with this church. Rev. Clarence Larkin, well known for his prophetic preaching and writings, had been a previous pastor. He was also linked with the early beginning of the Bible Institute of Pennsylvania. His biblical teachings had laid a strong foundation for the church.

When we became part of the fellowship, the pastor was Rev. August F. Ballbach, Sr. He had a pastor's heart and was a stalwart for the truth of God. Many came to Christ and a goodly number committed themselves to the Lord for service in His vineyard. Periodically, special evangelistic meetings were held. One campaign, held by Dr. Haikes, included a ministry of visitation outreach by the church members. The pastor's son, August, and Walter Angeny, both 11 years of age, were assigned to come to see me. They told me afterwards that when they approached my home, they lost their nerve and walked away. Later, no doubt under conviction, they came back and knocked on the door. Mother answered and the boys said they wanted to talk to me. I sat down with them in the parlor. I really don't remember all they said, other than that they asked me to accept Christ as my Savior. Without any hesitation I said I would. We got down on our knees and in childlike faith I confessed to the Lord Jesus that I was a sinner and I accepted Him as my personal Savior. I was only 12 years old but very conscious that something had taken place in my life and a peculiar joy flooded my heart. That same night I joined one of these boys on a visit to another boy's home, and we had the privilege of leading him to the Lord.

During my early high school years I lived a "Dr. Jekyll-Mr. Hyde" life style. I thought I had to live the Christian life in my own strength and struggled to do so, only to fail miserably. I was still part of the church and its activities—Junior choir, Boy's Club, the Young People's Society of which I became president. My life was enamored with sports—track, swimming, football, baseball, and basketball. I loved them all and trained diligently, always with the goal of winning. We formed a hometown athletic club and called it Fox Chase Foxes. It was made up of a fine group of high school-age fellows from various backgrounds. Two dislocated knees took me out of football action. It was hard to stand on the sidelines and watch. Periodically, I would get into the scrimmage only to end up with my knee going out. I finally had to give up and then became manager of the team. During this period of my life I was a worldly Christian, attending church but not living for the Lord even though I was the leader of the Young People's Society. The only one I was fooling was myself.

When dedicated Christians unite and become truly concerned for their young people, things are bound to happen as they did at Bethany Church. Bill Erwin, a staunch servant of the Lord, was my Sunday School teacher. He contributed much to the development of my Christian life. I admired Ed Castor, whom I called "Pop." He was a leader in the church, and a deep student of the Word. Dad Benner was one of the "older" deacons, a stalwart, kindly man of God. One day, a few years later, he confirmed my call to full-time service by telling me he felt that God had evidenced the fact that His hand was upon me. Elsie Sutton and Lilly Weimer were mature ladies who carried the young people on their hearts and were active in reaching out to us in many ways. God used home folks like these to mold my life. Their prayers were the effectual prayers of the righteous and they availed much.

These Christians formulated a group called "Life Service League." Their meetings were held on the first Saturday night of every month to stimulate commitment to the Lord and involvement in Christian service. Someone invited me to attend, but it meant a great sacrifice, for Saturday night was the time I had set aside for the glamor of the world and what it had to offer. However, I decided to go to one of the meetings to see what it was like. The first meeting impressed me. There was a fairly large group of young people and it was held in a home setting. We had fun, food, fellowship, and something challenging from the Word of God or a special testimony. As a result, I decided I would set aside that first Saturday of each month to attend Life Service League, and the rest of the Saturdays I continued to go out in the world. On one occasion, before going to Life Service League, I jokingly said to my mother, "Tonight I'm going to have 'Pop' Castor sing 'Saint Louie Blues.' " That revealed the attitude I had toward "Life Service" for the Lord. I am sure that all the group knew this and prayed more earnestly for me.

At each of these fellowship gatherings, everyone present gave a contribution of ten cents. This money was used to send a delegate to Keswick Young People's Victorious Life Conference in Whiting, New Jersey. As we neared the summer conference season, the group decided that we should choose our conference delegate from those who had never been to Keswick. A number of us qualified. Our names were all listed on a ballot, which was to be prayed over and voted upon at the next meeting. I wasn't excited about this and didn't have a desire to be chosen. When the votes were counted, everyone had voted for me except one, and that was the person I had voted for. They were unanimous that I should go.

After the results were announced, someone asked jubilantly, "Aren't you glad?" I tried to muster up an enthusiastic "Yeah." Inwardly, I was not as thrilled as everyone else seemed to be. They were happy because the Lord had answered their prayers. My idea of a Bible conference was a place where a lot of "old fogies" gathered to read their Bibles and stroke their beards. How could I get excited about that? The only compensating fact was that there would be swimming, canoeing, tennis, and other sports. Unfortunately, I would have to tell all the brawny athletes that I associated with that I was going to a Bible conference. I had no other choice but to go through with it. I learned later that Kitty (Pendleton) Brill, a member of the Life Service League, worked as a waitress at Keswick that summer and had the Keswick prayer group pray that I would be the delegate. They also prayed for me throughout the entire conference period.

I went to Keswick reluctantly and felt a bit sheepish upon my arrival. It was a Young People's Conference and the activities were geared accordingly. Hearing Addison Raws, the director, play his trumpet each morning was a moving experience. The food was good. Morning hours were devoted to Bible study and missionary messages. Dr. Robert McQuilkin spoke each day on "Victorious Christian Living" and he "batted" me all over the place. Dr. Dale spoke on missionary work in

Mexico, and Rev. Woodley from A.I.M. spoke on Africa. The Lord dealt with me throughout the week, and on Friday evening a special challenge was given for commitment of life.

I well remember walking down the aisle toward the front of the auditorium and that beautiful handpainted sign, right in the midst of the cedar trees that made up the background of the platform, with the challenging words, "For Me to Live is Christ ..." (Phil. 1:21). A number of other young people and I came forward and were dedicated to the Lord in prayer. I signed a decision card committing myself to the Lord, and in answer to the question as to whether I felt led to offer myself for missionary service, and if so, where, I wrote "Africa."

This was really the turning point in my life. The Lord enabled me to tell my athletic "buddies" about my decision. This was not easy but the Lord granted His help to maintain a good testimony. The whole direction of my life changed. I desired His purpose to be fulfilled in my life, namely,

> *I am crucified with Christ: nevertheless I live; yet not I, but Christ liveth in me: and the life which I now live in the flesh I live by the faith of the Son of God, who loved me, and gave Himself for me* (Galatians 2:20).

Chapter 3

The Master's Plan—
Is a Master Plan

I had outlined a plan for myself to eventually become a civil engineer, and I took the courses at Northeast High in Philadelphia with that goal in view. Drafting and drawing detailed mechanical plans were part of the course. Little did I realize, at that time, that the Master Draftsman had me on His drawing board, and He wanted me to hand over the designing of the plans to Him. Solomon stated, "A man's heart deviseth his way: but the Lord directeth his steps" (Prov. 16:9). Jeremiah knew that from experience when he said, "O Lord, I know that the way of man is not in himself: it is not in man that walketh to direct his step" (Jer. 10:23).

It is hard for our finite minds to grasp the fact that the Designer of the universe and all its facets of life wants us to yield control of our lives to Him. All His acts of creation were "very good" and so are His plans for us.

I completed high school during the depression years of the 1930's. Before pursuing further education I knew I would have to work for a period of time to obtain the finances I needed. I "pounded" the streets day by day and filled out scores of applications in an effort to secure any position or job that would produce an income. The procedure was routine and usually ended with the words, "If there are any openings we will get in touch with you." It was discouraging.

One day, toward the end of the summer months, I was chatting with a young man whom I had first met at the Life Service League. He was zealous for the Lord and spoke to our group on numerous occasions. I was, no doubt, attracted to him because his past way of life had been similar to mine. His name was Roy Brill. He had married Kitty Pendleton and together they had attended the Bible Institute of Pennsylvania. Roy and Kitty had graduated that year, 1931, and they were expecting to go to the National Bible Institute in New York to take a medical course in further preparation for service on the mission field. Roy had a student job at *The Philadelphia Evening Bulletin*. In our conversation Roy said he would give me his job if I would go to Bible school. Bible school never entered my mind but it sparked immediate interest. After I consulted Mother and Dad, it was agreed that I could accept the offer.

When the opening date for the B.I.O.P. came around, I enrolled as a student. I felt strange and was sure that all the other students were far superior to me in spiritual things. Most of them were older than I, and I was not too familiar with Bible studies, so it took a while to adjust to my new situation. The fact that Gordon Cook, one of my choice friends from

Bethany Baptist Church, was in my class was a real encouragement.

The Bible-centered curriculum was made up of various courses emphasizing a "Thus saith the Lord." We were taught not only to compare Scripture with Scripture but to compare our lives with Scripture! The godly lives of the professors and the testimonies of the founder, Dr. W.W. Rugh, and the Dean, Dr. L. Wade Gosnell, made a profound impression upon me. These were men who lived by faith and they were outstanding examples of what they taught.

I commuted to school each day. After school I went into the center of the city to work at the *Evening Bulletin*. I was happy with my routine. After approximately one month a crisis situation arose. The position that Roy Brill had handed over to me was considered, by the company, to be his personally, and could be allocated to another when he left. This is what took place, but now a new policy was initiated and all the job opportunities were placed under the jurisdiction of the school to assist resident students. This meant I no longer had a job, and with no income, my dad said I wouldn't be able to continue in school.

The depression of the 1930's was at its peak and the finances for daily public transportation were not available. I didn't know much about trusting the Lord, so I spoke to the Dean of Men, Dr. Kerns, concerning my plight. I told him I would have to terminate my studies because I would not have the trolley carfare for each day's travel. A short time after that conversation, the Dean called me aside and asked, "Will you come if you have the carfare?" I said that I would. Each week after that, an envelope containing a dollar was placed in my mailbox. This took care of all my travel, including my weekly practical Christian work assignment. Each week I ended up with ten cents left over, which I saved for unforeseen expenses. One week the dollar was not there so my savings bridged the gap, and the next week two dollars were in the envelope. To this day I don't know who made that God-given provision for me. I have often thought it might have been Dr. W.W. Rugh since he was sitting at his desk working when I explained my plight to Dean Kerns. He may have overheard my conversation and made the provision out of his own pocket. This is the kind of a man he was.

The depression began to take its toll on my dad. He was working only one or two days a week. At that time he decided to start a little grocery business. My sister and I sought to drum up trade by endeavoring to get our friends in the community to purchase butter, eggs, bacon, sausage, Philadelphia scrapple, ham, chickens, etc. We traveled miles by foot throughout the extended neighborhood. We took orders and then contacted the Armour and Swift Companies who delivered the goods to our home. The next two days were spent delivering to our faithful customers. Without a means of transportation, we delivered the orders with an old-time market basket carried on the arm. The business gradually grew and provided sufficient income to sustain the family. When the U.S. economy grew stronger, Dad went back to his usual work and my sister and I continued the grocery business. This is the way that our "Jehovah Jireh" (the Lord will provide) made provision for us and enabled me to complete my studies at the Bible Institute of Pennsylvania. Such experiences were all part of

God's plan to prepare me by teaching me to trust the Lord to meet my every need, no matter what the circumstances might be.

The daily study of the Scriptures made its impact upon my life and practical Christian work assignments were part of the Institute's program. These took the students to various city missions and brought us in contact with the reality of life and the consequences of the sins in the lives of those who were ensnared by the subtle temptations of the world, the flesh, and the devil. This was a new experience for me, and gradually the Lord implanted His constraining love within my heart with an attitude of "woe is me if I preach not the gospel." The thrill of leading people to the Lord was exhilarating. As my knowledge of the Lord and His Word grew, I was given opportunity to preach. In the summertime, we went out into the streets to herald the "glad tidings" in the highways and byways. Tract distribution afforded the opportunity of carrying on a friendly conversation with individuals in anticipation of leading them to the Lord.

The training that I received at the Institute, which later became Philadelphia College of Bible, found its way into the ministry of my home church, and our group of dedicated young people held meetings regularly in several city missions. In the summer months we held outdoor meetings on Friday evenings in the market place at 5th & Chew Streets, and on Saturday evenings in the center of our home town (Fox Chase). On Sunday afternoons we held forth in Burholme Park, singing and preaching to picnickers who gathered around. This was a stimulating experience and many came to the Savior.

During one summer, Roy Brill, Harry Crew, and I fixed up a Model-T Ford, loaded it with camping equipment and thousands of tracts and gospels, and made our way out to the Appalachian mountains of Pennsylvania. We went from town to town, door to door, witnessing and giving out literature. In some towns pastors invited us to hold meetings in their churches. We had a "shoestring" budget and our worn-out tires gave us a lot of trouble, but the purchase of several used spares carried us through. It was exciting to be a part of the action.

In the fall of 1933, I went to New York City to pursue a Missionary Medical Course at National Bible Institute, which later became Shelton College. Because I planned to work for my tuition and board, I arrived before the beginning of the school term. On my first night in the city, I had the privilege of speaking at a street meeting at Columbus Circle. The gentleman who had invited me and I made up the team. He had the permit and equipment, and I gave the message. It was exciting. I stood on a small stand in the midst of a crowd of a thousand or more and faced the competition of about ten other speakers who represented all sorts of causes, political and otherwise, such as The Association of Advancement of Atheism in America. As I remember, I spoke on "What think ye of Christ? Who do men say that I am?"

While I was a student at NBI, I spoke on many occasions from that same spot, as well as at Times Square. One night after two of us had the joy of leading someone to the Lord, our hearts were bubbling over with praise as we walked down Broadway on our way to the college. We were reminded of the literally thousands on

Missionary Medical students
National Bible Institute.

Broadway. They were seeking for what they thought was "life," but it was nothing compared to the thrill that we had in serving the One who said, "I am come that they might have life, and that they might have it more abundantly" (Jn. 10:10b).

Opportunities were afforded in churches and Sunday Schools. In one Sunday School they made up a class of all of the "rowdy" boys and asked me to teach it on a regular basis. In order to keep their attention, I spoke on some of the furious battles that took place in the Scriptures. The "punch line" was to give a spiritual application that would captivate their hearts.

The Missionary Medical Course was excellent and very concentrated. The classes were taught by top New York doctors. The practical application took place in the departmental dispensaries, the emergency ward, and operating room of Roosevelt Hospital and Bellevue Hospital. Anatomy, communicable diseases, obstetrics, dentistry, and nursing were just a few of the courses. I thoroughly enjoyed all this, even to the extent that I found myself evaluating all the symptoms that I might have! The course was good preparation for many problems that would confront missionaries in Africa.

My commitment to the Lord and to missionary work in Africa deepened during the time I was at NBI. I was looking to the Lord for guidance as to where I should serve in Africa and under which mission board. The Lord had His time for revealing this, and it happened one evening at a special missionary dinner at the college. Mrs. Marty Pontier of the Africa Inland Mission was the speaker. She had studied at NBI and had served for two terms in the Belgian Congo. Her husband, Rev. William Pontier, sat at a table with three of us fellows because he had to go out to another meeting later that evening. He was very personable and enthusiastic as he told about his ministry on the field and about the challenge of the unreached multitudes. As he spoke, something in my heart responded to all that he said, and I felt that this was the Lord's answer to my prayer for His guidance. From that time on I was convinced that this was God's call to Congo and to the A.I.M.

Immediately after graduation, I sent a letter of inquiry to Rev. Henry Campbell, the General Secretary of A.I.M. in the United States, and I also had a personal interview with him, which was very encouraging. He felt that since I lived in Philadelphia, I should proceed with my application by contacting Pastor Hoag of Barachah Church, who was the Secretary of the A.I.M. Philadelphia Committee. This brought me in contact with the committee, which consisted of about ten outstanding godly Christian men. Some were pastors and others were business and professional men. Dr. Kantz, a dentist, was chairman.

Every month I met with them, together with furloughed missionaries. This fellowship gave me the opportunity to feel the pulse of the A.I.M. and their practical and prayerful concern for the missionaries and their ministries, as well as the problems they faced on the field. It revealed a deep family relationship and love that made me more desirous to belong to such a team. I rejoiced when I received the news of my acceptance.

Waiting on the Lord for financial support was a valuable spiritual exercise. This was all a part of His preparation.

Working at America's Keswick in 1935, as part of the summer staff under the leadership of Dr. Addison Raws and Carl Pfoust, plus the stimulus of the Word of God given by the conference Bible teachers and missionaries, helped to strengthen my faith to trust the Lord for all my needs.

Following my ordination to the ministry, I felt constrained to pray for the Lord to send me out in November, 1935. Three weeks before the outgoing missionary party was scheduled to leave on November 20th, I still needed $800 before I could join them. That was a lot of money during the depression years. My dear dad, who at that time was not fully committed to the Lord, said I was crazy to think I would get the eight hundred dollars as he himself had to work a long time for that amount. The Lord by His grace sent in every penny. The night before I was to leave for New York, our home was filled with friends who had come to bid me farewell. Dad openly stated that he had said I was crazy to think I could get the money needed in such a short time, but he had seen the Lord perform a miracle.

A large crowd of friends came to see the 12 missionaries off on the *S.S. Deutschland*. In the main lounge of the ship, Mr. Jacob Stam conducted a service that was a real testimony. My mother was making the trip with me to England, her first visit in 25 years. It was hard saying good-bye to my dad and sister. As I hugged Dad, through the tears, I said, "Dad, come out and out for the Lord." My sister wrote that the following Wednesday Dad was in the church prayer meeting. He stood up and gave a heartwarming testimony. From that time on he continued to go on with the Lord in a wonderful way.

I spent a week in England with Mother, visiting relatives. This was a new experience for me because we did not have any in the U.S.A. Some did not know the Lord and it was a privilege to witness to them.

The party of missionaries continued on to Germany and I joined them when they came back on the *S.S. Wangoni* to Southampton. My mother and her sister, Aunt Annie, came to see me off. This parting was most difficult. The last earthly view I had of Mom was on the Southampton docks where, with deep tearful emotion, she bade her only son farewell. I can still see her as the ship pulled away. It is not only the missionary who experiences stress at the time of departure, but the family and loved ones who are left behind share equally in the sacrifice that is made. Thank God, they shall someday share in the "dividing of the spoil."

Traveling by ship was slow, but it gave opportunity for sight-seeing in the various Mediterranean ports of call. Our first touch with Africa took place in Tunisia, with its colorful Arab setting, but so difficult to reach for Christ. Then we went on to Genoa, Alexandria, Port Said, the Suez Canal, and the Red Sea.

On Christmas Eve, the *Wangoni* plowed its way through a rather rough Red Sea. I attended a special captain's Christmas service that had been arranged by the officers of the ship. One of our fellow traveling missionaries, Rev. Brinkert from Germany, was asked to speak. He was a staunch evangelical. Speaking in German, he gave a powerful message as he told about the birth of Christ and the purpose for which He came. Later in the evening the captain, wanting to show the holiday spirit, offered free liquor to the men of the crew. Several hours later the crew was in a drunken brawl.

All the missionaries were in a meeting together in a small room that had been assigned to us for times of fellowship and prayer. We rejoiced in the great gift of God's only begotten Son and that we were on our way to Africa to proclaim this message. While we were in prayer, suddenly the engines of the ship went silent. A few moments later a steward made his appearance in our room to announce that someone had fallen overboard, and the captain wanted everyone to report to the main deck in order to check on all the passengers and to see who was missing.

They soon found out that it was one of the crew members. The ship was backed up some distance to where they thought he had fallen into the sea and floodlights lit up the area. Lifeboats were lowered and some of the more sober crew men manned these boats, but their search was in vain. I remember that when some of the more drunken crew members were able to grasp the fact that one of their shipmates had fallen overboard, they frantically strove against those who withstood them as they tried to throw themselves over the rail into the sea to search for their lost colleague. In reality, these men did not have the ability to save their friend. They only had a hazy view and foggy knowledge of how to rescue the one who was lost. After a long period of time and futile effort, the ship pulled away from the sad scene, leaving only a burning buoy as a possible signal of refuge in case the lost crewman was still alive. It left me feeling a great sense of loss because a soul had, no doubt, gone out into a Christless eternity.

The drunken sailors' hazy view of meeting the need of their lost friend reminded me of the hazy view and foggy knowledge that many within the Church of Christ have concerning the needs of a lost and dying world. The apostle Paul shook the shoulder of the Corinthian church to remind them of this, "Awake to righteousness [or come out of your drunken stupor], and sin not; for some have not the knowledge of God: I speak this to your shame" (1 Cor. 15:34). It is high time that we return to sober thinking concerning meeting the needs of a lost and dying world.

On Christmas Day I had the privilege of speaking at a service for the passengers. It was a serious time of reflection as we told them of God's great gift, "For God so loved the world, that He gave His only begotten Son..." (Jn. 3:16) and, to make what He accomplished in dying for our sins to become a reality, the "gift" must be received personally by faith. The result is the forgiveness of sins and life everlasting.

Shortly after our departure from Port Sudan, I came down with pneumonia and remained in the ship's hospital bay for the next week. Paul Lehrer, the only other man in our party, was a great blessing to me, and fellow missionaries prayed earnestly. God answered and I was able to get up the day before we landed at Mombasa, our port of debarkation. When we arrived I was "weak as a kitten" but gradually regained my strength.

We proceeded overnight by a slow train, three hundred miles to Nairobi, which was a small growing city, and then on to the A.I.M. Kijabe station. There, in the home of Dr. and Mrs. Elwood Davis, I was nurtured back to normal health. After a week, those of us who were heading for the Belgian Congo continued our journey by train overland, by boat over Lake Kioga, by bus to Butiaba, and again by boat across Lake Albert to Port Mahagi on the bordering shores of the Congo. We were met there by Leonard Buyse, who finally got us through customs and immigration about 9:00 p.m. It was then I met Emil Suwylka, one of A.I.M.'s pioneers from Tanganyika. We rode on top of the baggage in the back of the truck while the ladies in our party rode in the cab. We slowly climbed up the winding escarpment road to the six-thousand-foot altitude of Rethy station. It was 2:00 a.m. when we arrived, and we were given a very warm welcome by Mr. and Mrs. Norman Camp, Sr., who provided us with a hearty meal, even at that hour.

Roy and Kitty Brill.

During my first week in Congo I was brought in contact with nearly all the A.I.M. Congo missionaries. They had come together from their stations several hundred miles away, and from Uganda and French Equatorial Africa, for a week of conference. It was a privilege to meet our A.I.M. family. Some had served the Lord for many years and had laid a solid foundation for the Church of Christ in Congo. It was a thrill to see Roy and Kitty Brill, who had meant so much to me. My arrival was an answer to their years of faithfully upholding me in prayer. Beginning my missionary career at a Bible conference was ideal. Emil Suwylka, a rugged godly pioneer, was the conference speaker. He spoke out of his heart from the Scriptures and practical experiences. He made one statement with reference to the necessity of maintaining a vibrant prayer life that made an impact on me. Speaking of one of his Tanganyika colleagues, Thomas Marsh, he said, "The patches on the knees of that man's pants spoke glory to the Lord." This instruction meant much to me as a young missionary. It was the Lord's briefing and orientation before going into the conflict.

During that conference I met with the Congo Field Council and was assigned to Aba station to study Bangala and eventually be responsible for the 75 "Chapel Bush Schools" manned by Congolese evangelists.

Chapter 4

Assignment: Bush

Aba was that little dot on the northeastern corner of the Congo map. It was a very beautiful and fertile area bordering on the Sudan. Scrub forests covered vast areas and savannah grasslands provided farmland that produced abundant crops for the massive tribal population. It was four degrees north of the equator at an altitude of four thousand feet. The rainy season provided a comfortable climate that lasted six months, and the dry season started in December, getting progressively hotter during the next six months.

The Mission station was located on a rocky hill that could be seen from miles around. To the Africans it was known as Nyanyala, which means "at the foot of it there is blessing." This described the lush, well-watered farming area surrounding the base of the hill. From its summit one could look out over the rolling plains for nearly 50 miles and see hundreds of villages scattered throughout the countryside. This was our "Macedonia" with literally hundreds of thousands of people for whom Christ died.

Aba station has a rich history. It was a stepping-stone in the Mission front line of advance. It was chosen as the headquarters for the existing five fields of A.I.M. by Rev. Charles Hurlburt, who had been the General Director. His goal was to reach Chad, the fulfillment of the vision of Peter Cameron Scott, the founder of the A.I.M.

When I arrived, various phases of missionary work were already being carried out. This work included a large medical work that ministered to thousands, a Bible school, a boys' school, a girls' school, a women's school, a printing press, etc. It was also the base of operations for the Congo Field Director, Rev. George Van Dusen.

The missionaries and the thousand or more Africans who resided on the station gave me a warm welcome. Roy Brill, who had played such an important part in my life, was station superintendent and very supportive in getting me established and oriented to "bush work." He and his wife, Kitty, helped this bachelor get settled in my own house and thoughtfully provided me with a good cook, Gidona Yebe. Abarama Diliwa and Matatiya cared for household chores, which included washing and ironing clothes. For all of which I was most thankful. We became strong friends and Yebe and Abarama were part of my team for 18 years. The home of Roy and Kitty was a place of warmhearted fellowship and encouragement during those early days of adjustment to new things in a strange land.

Language study was the first order of business. Mabel Gingrich, my tutor, had years of experience and was an excellent teacher. She had charge of a large boys' school, and she had a great love for the African people. At first language study seemed like a laborious struggle, but it gradually blossomed into reality. Traveling out in the "bush" alone and being surrounded by African helpers stimulated progress. The constant repetition of words, phrases, and sentence syntax helped the language to become a part of me until gradually I found myself actually thinking in Bangala. It was essential that I obtain an intimate knowledge of the language since this was essential to learning the culture of those to whom I would be ministering.

Life out in the "bush" became an exciting experience. At first, though, I felt very strange in a culture that was different, and my limited vocabulary made it difficult to enter into warmhearted fellowship. But as time passed and experience increased, so did an intimate relationship with the national brethren. I soon found that many of them had spiritual depth and were zealous in their service for the Lord. They had a good sense of humor, which many times gave way to rollicking laughter when I joked with them.

I am grateful that my assignment was to minister to the people who lived in the "bush." To me it was the front line of advance into enemy territory, challenging hearts with the message that "is the power of God unto salvation" (Rom. 1:16) and seeing God work. Aba Church was responsible for a vast area covering about 150 miles along the Congo border where there were hundreds of villages. Many of these villages had no permanent witness, but some had African pastor-evangelists whose congregations varied in size. The church building was also used as a school throughout the week, and the pastor became the teacher.

Living in the villages brought me close to the hearts of the people and exposed me to their culture and way of life. This varied to some degree according to the tribes; there were at least ten in our area. I found the African people warm in their friendship and very family-orientated. They were also members of an extended family, which developed into a clan, glued together by a strong loyalty. The father of the household was the patriarch. Since his wife was purchased with a dowry, she became part of his clan. They greatly loved their children. Together, the family became a working team, each assigned to specific duties. Farming took pre-eminence because their lives depended upon their crops. From the beginning to the end of the rainy season they could all be found out in their gardens, working from early in the morning to late in the afternoon, hoeing, harrowing, and hopefully, reaping a good harvest. The boys worked with father, helping him dig. The girls worked with mother, breaking the clods of earth to prepare the soil for planting. Many times large family groups joined together to dig each other's gardens, to the rhythm of an African song, after which they ended the day with a jubilant feast. The father and son also cared for the domestic animals, goats, sheep, or cattle. Mother and daughter were responsible for firewood and water, as well as the preparation of the family meals and, of course, the care of the babies.

The evening meal was a welcome time after a hard day of work. The family huddled around a huge plate of "ugali," which consisted of thickly cooked cassava, corn, or millet flour. It was eaten with goat or wild meat, chicken, or maybe just spinach cooked with peanut butter. Africans are very hospitable; missionaries were cordially invited to be their guests and were treated royally. The meal began and ended with the washing of hands. Their mealtimes were generally filled with light talk and much laughter.

Building their mud and wattle-thatched homes was a family project. These houses were about 20 feet square, divided into several rooms. A limited amount of handmade furniture made up the furnishings. Just a short distance behind their home was a cook-house, which was mother's workshop. Then, a good distance behind that, was the "little house" or "outside plumbing." All of this made up "home, sweet home."

During the early days, before the arrival of colonial governments, their homes dotted the countryside with family groups living in close proximity to each other. After the Belgian government took control of the Congo, they sought to congregate all the various clans in street-like villages. This was done to facilitate governing and caring for the medical needs of the people. Each village was supervised by a "headman" who, in turn, was responsible to a regional sub-chief who came under the supervision of the Paramount Chief of the tribe. In actuality this was the pattern of tribal rulership that existed long before the arrival of the colonial government.

Generally, the people lived peaceably together, but occasionally contention arose when goats destroyed someone's garden or when a person was injured in a family squabble or drunken brawl. Sometimes the village tranquility was disturbed when someone claimed that a sickness or a death in their family was caused by a curse and everyone was afraid that they might be accused. Such cases necessitated lengthy investigations, which sometimes included sorcery. Petty violations were handled by the "headman" or sub-chief, but major crimes were generally judged by the Paramount Chief and the elders of the tribe. As I lived and moved among the people, they became a part of me. Their joys, burdens, frustrations, and heart-aches became a part of my life. These were the "other sheep" the Lord said He must also bring (Jn. 10:16). They were the people to whom I was called. They were loved by God, and He gave me His constraining love for them.

Partners in outreach.

Only a month after I arrived at Aba station, while I was still in the process of getting settled in, I came down with a fever that was routinely treated for malaria. However, it was finally diagnosed as amoebic dysentery. I was confined to the Aba hospital and wonderfully cared for by Dr. and Mrs. Kleinschmidt. I slowly responded to the treatment and, although weakened in body, I gradually regained my strength.

I anticipated my first safari alone, even before I knew the language, with excitement. Of course, I also had a measure of apprehension about entering into that

Ready for safari.

which was new and yet unknown, at least as far as my own experience was concerned. All my camping gear, bedding, food, and literature was packed in five or six bundles carried by porters. These porters were young men from the tribe and they changed as we went from village to village. I traveled by bicycle, together with an African pastor, and our destination was the village of Chief Ali. He gave me a very warm welcome and showed a keen interest in the things of the Lord, although at that time he was not a Christian. The two-week period that I spent there was a learning experience. The villagers crowded in a large chapel in the village to listen to the African pastor holding forth the Word of Life. My knowledge of the language was very limited at the time, but I could enter into the enthusiastic zeal of the preacher and the joyful singing of the congregation. The people were very friendly and gave me a hearty welcome. The absence of a translator on this trip was, in some respects, actually a blessing because it made me use the few words that I did know to ask, "What is this? What is that?" and I found the Africans most desirous to help me. When they gave me the answer, I repeated it and thus increased my vocabulary. This was the beginning of a ministry that would bring me into close touch with various African tribes and their cultures. This was wonderful preparation for the years ahead.

A safari in the African bush was always an adventure. I bicycled the narrow African footpaths, well-worn by those who traveled from village to village.

Crossing river on swinging bridge.

Sometimes there were many miles of paths between the villages that took me through the wilderness of tall elephant grass or semi-woodland areas, or slogging through a swamp. At times it was necessary to swim across small rivers or cross larger ones on V-shaped monkey-vine bridges swaying in the breeze. Many times I traveled alone, and on other occasions with African pastors. There were times when the silence was broken by the thrashing of a wild animal in the brushland. It could be a friendly bush buck scampering off or it might be an unfriendly bush buffalo getting ready for a possible confrontation. Often I came across the fresh tracks of animals, even those of a lion, but fortunately I did not have any encounters. When I arrived at the village of my destination, the head man or village chief greeted me warmly and made arrangements for me to set up my camping gear in one of the mud-thatched dwellings.

The people of the Logo tribe were farmers. Each family group went out to their garden early in the morning at six o'clock, even mother with a baby upon her back. They worked hard throughout the day and at about five o'clock in the afternoon, they made their way back to their humble homes. This was the time I started down the village street to give them greetings. I shook hands with father, mother, and all the little tots. I told the mothers how nice and fat her little baby was, which always rejoices a mother's heart. I talked with the father and I asked him how his crops were growing, since they were the lifeline of their

Hut to hut visitation.

existence. At the opportune moment, I gave them the gospel in simple terms, using illustrations they could understand.

Portering safari equipment.

An African evangelist, Eliya Mandema, taught me how to convey the message within the context of the culture of his people. This was most helpful and a very important part of my training for bush ministry. Thus, I went from hut to hut and person to person until about eight o'clock in the evening, when I finished "fine-combing" the village with the message of the gospel.

Then I returned to the mud hut where I was staying. There, my African cook prepared my evening meal. After that time of refreshment, I came out and sat near an open fire with all the men and boys of the village gathered around. The women and girls huddled around another fire close by. We welcomed the warmth of the fire, especially during the cool evenings of the rainy season. Even the village dogs crawled up as close as they could to the fire. This was a wonderful experience, sitting out under the starry galaxies of the southern hemisphere and listening to some of the elders repeat the folklore stories that had been passed from father to son down through many generations. It was a time of getting to know them and of learning of their way of life. I always used such occasions to continue to press home the claims of Christ upon their lives.

Encountering elephant grass.

One evening while relaxing by the fire, and enjoying each other's company, suddenly we heard the sound of the tom-toms in some far-off village. I turned to Yokana, the African pastor who was with me, and asked "Azi kula nini pai kuna?"—"What is taking place over there?"

After listening for a moment, he said, "There are no horns or flutes accompanying the beating of those drums, so that means there is death in yonder village."

Those drums continued their monotonous and dismal intonations throughout the night, accompanied by the death chants of loved ones who had been left behind. It was an experience that really burdened my heart for the needs of the people who were without Christ, even to the extent that I longed to impart unto them the knowledge of the God of all comfort known only through our Lord and Savior Jesus Christ. On such occasions I often retired only to hear those drums still dolefully sending forth their uncanny melody throughout the hours of the night. Often, as I awoke, I bowed in prayer before the Lord of the harvest, beseeching Him that these benighted souls might know Him.

Securing make-shift bridge.

It was then I realized this was the result of the systems of worship that man had erected according to the standards of his own vain reasoning. Solomon rightly said, "There is a way which seemeth right unto a man, but the end thereof are the ways of death" (Prov. 14:12). I was reminded that our safaris into the bushland areas of Africa were in reality journeys into darkness. I was also mindful of the fact that God, in His yearning for all mankind, has always given a witness to the men of all ages revealing the wonders of His power, glory, and majesty throughout all His creation. Thus, He has left them without an excuse.

However, instead of accepting God's revelation, the tendency of the heart of man is to forsake the ways of the Lord and the consequence is that men's "senseless hearts are darkened" and thus they change the glory of the incorruptible God into an image. Out of their darkened hearts evolve the worship of dead images made like unto man and birds and four-footed beasts and creeping things. In that men love darkness rather than light God gave them up and gives them over to the darkness of their own hearts. Living in the villages of Africa, I could feel "the power of darkness" and I saw those who were bound by "the chains of darkness." My heart ached for them, that they might know Him the "Light of the world."

Dr. and Mrs. Ralph Kleinschmidt—Aba.

One day, as Dr. Kleinschmidt and I entered the village of Yeyowa, we were informed by the village chief that a young man had just died. Of course, doctor was immediately interested in the cause of his death. We walked down the long village street to the place where a large group of mourners had gathered. After greeting them, we told them that doctor would like to examine the body of the young man and we were given permission to go into the little mud hut where the corpse lay.

We bent low beneath the grass eaves of the roof and went in through the small entrance. After our eyes became accustomed to the darkness of the windowless mud building, we could see the form of the one who had gone out into eternity upon the floor. As we entered, his elderly mother was bent over his body, going through her incantations, but when she saw us she stopped. There was a smoldering fire off to one side giving forth quite a bit of smoke, which made its way up to the thatched roof and out the best way it could. We noted that there were sorrowing loved ones standing around in that rotund hut. Doctor bent over the form of the young man and examined his body meticulously. Following the examination, both doctor and I had the opportunity to give them the gospel and tell them about the love of God who sent His only begotten Son to die and pay the penalty for their sins, in order that He might take them to His eternal heavenly village where there is no more sorrow, pain, or death. We left with heavy hearts. As we went out, the elderly mother again bent over the form of her son, waving her body back and forth to the rhythm of her own death chant. The power and chains of darkness were very much in evidence. Mourning for this family would not cease at the time of burial. Each morning from four o'clock until sunrise they would gather to sing their songs of woe. Again we were reminded, this was the result of the systems of worship that man had erected according to the standards of his own vain reasoning. The voice of Jeremiah the prophet echoes down through the corridors of time with the solemn words, "O Lord, I know that the way of man is not in himself: It is not in man that walketh to direct his steps" (Jer. 10:23).

Africans are very conscious of the presence and power of death. When death takes a great toll in a village,

Dental extraction.

they may move their entire village from one location to another. They will explain that their departed ancestors were not happy with the place they had chosen for their previous village and therefore, by means of divination, they had sought a new site. However, death still stalks them as they move from place to place. Many times they give names to their children that bespeak death. At the time of a death, the African women let out a very mournful, weird, and blood-curdling sound known as the "death wail." It is somewhat like a yodel, going high and low, almost reaching the point of being a scream. Sometimes entire villages join their voices bemoaning the loss of a loved one.

One day, as I rode into a village on my bicycle, I was confronted by a heart-rending scene of a mother standing upon a mound of the freshly-made grave of her son, who had been gored to death by a buffalo. Her hands were stretched toward the heavens and she was letting out the death wail again and again in a tireless fashion. I turned to the evangelist who was with me and asked him if they had any interpretation in their tribal tongue for the sounds she was uttering. His response was a pathetic "no." We both knew that these sounds bespoke the anguish of a bereft heathen heart, but some missionary has rightfully defined them as meaning, "no hope." That places a different interpretation upon that entire scene of the mother with her hands uplifted toward the heavens crying, "No hope, no hope, no hope."

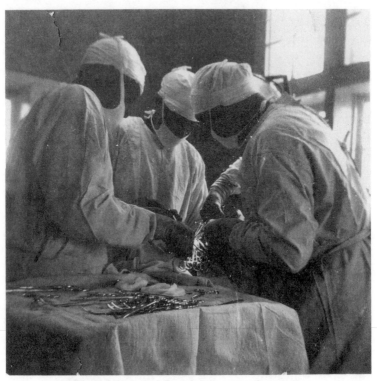

In surgery with African assistants.

As the Scripture says, "Without Christ...having no hope, and without God in the world" (Eph. 2:12). What an epitaph for the grave of anyone who goes out into a Christless eternity: "It is appointed unto men once to die, but after this the judgment" (Heb. 9:27), and "Except a man be born again, he cannot see the kingdom of God" (Jn. 3:3b).

The contrast of the fruits of darkness and light are seen and felt very vividly at funeral services in Africa. I was in the village of Paramount Chief Dramba at the time of his death. He had been witnessed to on many occasions, but never accepted Christ as his Savior. The elders of the tribe and his extended family (he had eighteen wives), would demand judgment on those responsible for the curse that brought about his death. The elderly women of the village feared that they would be accused; therefore, they must show by vigorous action that they were not the culprits. To prove their point, they prepared a deep muddy pit and actually did handsprings into this muddy mass, smearing it all over their bodies. They did this to escape a possibly horrible death. They might be forced to drink the poison cup, which they say declares their guilt or innocence. Watching such a scene moves one's heart with compassion toward them.

The burial scene of one who knows the Lord is altogether different. Loved ones and friends gather by the graveside, sorrowing not as those who have no hope, but sympathizing with the family over the departure of one who was dearly loved. The songs of Zion are sung and the Word of God is given to comfort broken hearts. The gospel is proclaimed to those who are not Christians, and at such a time as this grieving hearts are turned to joy for those who respond by receiving Christ as their Savior.

It was for this purpose that, as an ambassador of the King of kings and Lord of lords, I went forth with the message of hope for those who have no hope, so that "The people which sat in darkness saw a great light; and to them which sat in the region and shadow of death light is sprung up" (Mt. 4:16). Only one message is able to pierce the darkness of heathenism, and that is the gospel of light. Only one Person is able to break the shackles of the god of this world, and that is Jesus, the One who said, "I have come into the world as a light, so that no one who believes in Me should stay in darkness" (Jn. 12:46 NIV).

Chapter 5

Beneath the Congo Moon

I was happy in my bush ministry but one thing was missing—a helpmate! Over a period of time, trekking to the villages got lonely. Even the Lord was mindful of this, when He said, "It is not good for the man to be alone. I will make a helper suitable for him" (Gen. 2:18 NIV). So I earnestly prayed the bachelor's prayer: "Lord, send the helpmate that is suitable for me." I prayed this before going to the field and for more than a year during my "bushland" experience. The Psalmist said, "I will order my prayer to thee and eagerly watch" (Ps. 5:3 NAS) or "…wait in expectation" (Ps. 5:3 NIV). So I prayed and eagerly watched and waited in expectation!

Finally the day dawned and Jennie Long arrived at Aba from the United States with two other young ladies to be assigned by the Field Council, which was in session. Our first casual meeting was at the station noonday prayer meeting, after which Mabel Gingrich, one of the senior missionaries, quietly gave me some motherly advice in her very unique, slow-spoken drawl, "Now, Sid, take your pick!"

Jennie and her girls' school.

In the providence of God, Jen was assigned to take charge of the girls' boarding school at Aba after a period of language study and observation of the girls' work at Aru station, 110 miles away. Returning to Aba, she continued her language study and cultural adaptation and was quickly initiated into the routine of the work. There were about 50 single girls in the "girls' home," ranging in age from 10 to 20. Most of them had come from distant villages, and Aba became their "home" where they lived, worked, studied, and played. They came from different tribes to obtain a Christian education. Each day started with morning prayers, then most of them were off to work in the school gardens. Throughout the morning Jen taught six of the more advanced girls, who were teachers, and prepared them to conduct the afternoon classes.

As a new missionary, Jen soon found out that she needed to learn a great deal about the African way of life. It was only natural for the girls to try all their tricks on the new "*madamo.*" It was not always easy to

Jennie with her teachers.

distinguish the guilty party, since at first they all looked alike and each had several names that could be changed whenever it was expedient to do so. She soon found out that they were jovial and could laugh heartily. When there was a full moon, she would join them in the evening, singing and playing games. A bond of love was formed that continued in the years that followed.

As time went on, Jen and I had contacts with each other at social events with our station missionaries and thus our friendship began to grow. Concerning that which took place from then on, even Solomon in all his wisdom revealed that he was amazed and couldn't understand "...the way of a man with a maid" (Prov. 30:19c). Even the tennis court was refurbished so that we could play out our "love" game!

Courting in Africa had to be carried out in a far different manner than in our homeland. It had to be contextualized, that is, within the context of the African culture. It wasn't wise to go to places alone. We couldn't hold hands because it was not permitted in tribal traditions. We wanted to maintain a strong Christian testimony; therefore, whenever we went anywhere together, we took an African along with us. On one occasion, we planned a little picnic out on "the road to Sudan." I needed gasoline for my car and knew that I could get some from George Van Dusen, our Congo Field Director, who was based at Aba. I wrote a note to ask him for gas and let him know that I was taking Miss Long for a picnic—to do personal work! He sent the gas and wrote that he would be praying for big results "in your personal work."

When a young man's heart is full of love, he searches for ways to express it, by going out to dinner together or to a concert. And, of course, there must be "love gifts."

However, in our remote area, things like this were practically impossible. But love finds a way to create its own channels of expression. I didn't have any beautiful flowers in my garden, but I did have succulent vegetables. So, I filled a basket with the best of the land and sent it to Jen by the hand of my faithful African helper. He was aware of what was going on, and he was delighted to be a bearer of gifts of love. He returned with some candies Jen had brought from the States, but he had a sad expression on his face. Jen had chosen the amount of vegetables she thought she could use and returned the rest. He thought that I had been jilted since, according to African culture, the whole gift must be accepted!

On one occasion, Jen's short-wave radio needed some adjusting and I willingly volunteered my expertise! All the adjustments were made in such a way that my signals would come through loud and clear. I wanted to make sure that her set was so "fine tuned" that she would be able to zero in on my "wavelength."

The 13 missionaries at Aba Mission station formed a very close community. You can be sure that all were sympathetic and greatly interested. They were spectators who excitedly watched every action and inwardly cheered as we played out our love game. They encouraged Jen and me by inviting us to their homes for meals and, most of all, they prayed for us.

After a dinner at the Van Dusen home, Jen and I walked down the Aba hill road. It was a beautiful evening in October and about halfway down we stopped. In the distance, little fires indicated villages. Families were relaxing around the fires following a hard day's work in their gardens. But to me, the full moon was more evident, radiant in all its glory. It seemed as though the galaxies of the southern hemisphere were more brilliant than ever. The scenario was ordered of the Lord. I asked the right question and Jen gave the right answer! Then I struggled to wax poetic: "Beneath the Congo moon she stood." While I was searching for exotic and exciting words that would rhyme, Jen's humor got the best of her and she blurted out, "The village cow!" We soon announced our engagement to our missionary colleagues, and the Congo Field Council granted permission to proceed with our plans for the wedding.

In the meantime, both of us carried on with our ministries. I made my next trip into the bush with a light heart, and while on that safari I penned the following verse:

"Darling Jennie"

'Twas at a place called Aba,
In far-off Congo land,
That by God's grace I met her,
For it was in His plan.

My prayers had oft ascended,
The girl, Thy choice, please send;
And in His love He answered.
The best He did intend.

If words could but describe her,
Too poor they seem to be,
Most beautiful and lovely,
E'en these come short you see.

Many things the Lord did use
To make our hearts both one
And truly we do thank Him,
For 'tis what He has done.

How vegetables show romance,
  I'm sure I do not know;
Love must have a score of ways
  And thus her seed doth sow.

Radio is marvellous,
  Everyone will admit
E'en to this poor technician
  A new "wavelength" did exist.

Tennis even had a part,
  For when it didn't rain,
We went acourting on the court,
  To play out our love game.

For "twitters" in our romance,
  And times of nervous strain,
Beloved fellow workers
  Were more than once to blame.

One evening in October,
  Beneath the Congo moon,
My love, made known to Jennie,
  And that was none too soon.

I love you, Jennie, love you,
  And trust 'tis plain to see,
So for the day I'm praying,
  That soon my wife you'll be.

My heart's just overflowing,
  As this poem I write,
For 'tis but a beginning
  Of a happy married life.

With all that is within me,
  I praise His holy name,
And may our lives together
  Forever Christ proclaim.

With only several months left before the wedding, we joyously made arrangements for the big event. Could we accomplish all that needed to be done before the January date? We informed our parents by cable and Jen's mother immediately sent out a wedding dress. The wedding rings were purchased by a friend in the homeland with the last eight dollars I had in my bank account! Unfortunately, my missionary income couldn't afford a diamond.

January 22, 1938, dawned with all the glory of a beautiful, sunny, dry-season day. We stayed at Aru Mission station just across the border from the small town of Arua in Uganda. Our friends, Mr. and Mrs. Guilding,

pioneer missionaries, escorted us to the British District Commissioner's office for the official service; his name was "Slaughter"! In the presence of his wife, the Guildings and Doris Groat, with true British dignity, the ceremony was performed and we committed ourselves to each other as life partners. This was only the beginning of our wedding formalities. We now had to cross back into the Congo and then drive south 150 miles to our station of Rethy, nestled in the beautiful rolling hills that rise

Here comes the bride.

sixty-five hundred feet above Lake Albert (Mobutu). More than one hundred missionaries were gathered there for their biannual conference, already in session.

The missionaries had joyfully prepared for the wedding before our arrival. It was mid-afternoon when we reached Rethy, and we had to get cleaned up from the dusty, dry-season roads and get dressed for the occasion. It was about five o'clock in the afternoon when all the missionaries gathered on the spacious lawn in front of the home of Leonard Buyse. The ceremony took place in front of a gorgeous lavender bougainvillea-covered arbor with countless blossoms in full bloom. The bridal party consisted of Doris Groat, the maid of honor; Claudon Stauffacher, the best man; Faith Windsor, a lovely flower girl; Helen and Ruth Buyse, two cute little sisters who carried the train of

Our wedding at Congo Missionary Conference.

the bridal veil, and David Amstutz, the ring bearer. Rev. George Van Dusen, our Field Director, performed the religious ceremony. A small pump organ was the only musical instrument. Each of us came in and took our places before the arbor. Then, to the strains of "Here Comes the Bride," my beautiful bride appeared in her lovely wedding gown and we entered into our solemn vows before the Lord and to each other for life.

The dining hall was festively decorated and there was even a three-tier wedding cake that was masterfully designed by Harold Amstutz. Our mission family went all out to make this a wonderful occasion.

I knew that some of the men were planning to rig my car to keep us from getting away on our honeymoon; therefore, I arranged with Bill Pontier to borrow his car. We also avoided the roadblocks they set up and continued happily on our way, 250 miles south through the giant mahogany trees of the Ituri forest

Honeymoon trip through Ituri Forest.

and rolling volcanic hills to Lake Kivu, the highest navigable lake in Africa.

We had made arrangements with friends connected with the Swedish Mission to stay at their mission station located on the banks of the lake. There were no missionaries there. It was a beautiful spot with all sorts of tropical flowers and fruit growing out of black volcanic ash. Swimming and canoeing in a dugout canoe were all part of our daily routine of leisure.

Honeymoon cottage—Lake Kivu.

After several days, however, our tranquility was disturbed early one afternoon. One of the African caretakers of the property announced that the "fire of Satan" had started. He took us to a hill just behind the grass-roofed house and pointed to a small cloud of smoke some distance away. I was not impressed because we had come from north of the equator where dry-season fires were very much in evidence. However, this was the rainy season for Kivu. Everything was green and in full bloom, but that fact never entered my mind. Therefore

I said, "Oh, that is nothing to be concerned about," and dismissed it from my thoughts. Around 5:30 p.m. the same man appeared to announce that he and others were leaving. I asked, "Why?"

He said, "Because of the fire of satan," and pointed up into the sky that now had a glowing red appearance. I asked him if it would come here and he assured me that it would.

"Will it burn the grass roof?"

"Yes."

I said to Jen, "We had better go."

We hurriedly packed our panel delivery Ford and took off with the African as our guide. The roads were crowded with people leaving the area. Men and women were carrying as many of their precious possessions as they could on their heads and under their arms. Goats were hurried along the road and chickens were carried in baskets. All were fleeing for their lives from the "fire of satan." All were aware of the fact from stories that had been passed down through generations, that years before, Mt. Nyamlagira had erupted and spewed its molten lava several thousand feet into the air, taking the lives of hundreds of villagers and destroying their homes and crops. The effect was still very much in evidence. Black volcanic ash and cinders were everywhere.

We drove to the small town of Saki to investigate how serious this really was. We found the Greek merchants piling merchandise into their trucks to move out of the area. A special car had been sent in to rescue the Belgian District Commissioner. This indicated that we should continue on as fast as we could, especially since darkness was approaching. The narrow road we took was curving and precipitous. Generally, a warning was given to all who decided to take it, but the police guard had also fled so we were not aware of the danger. The heavens were growing more red by the minute, and this increased as darkness enveloped us. We tried to travel in haste, but we soon realized that the winding road had to be negotiated with much care or we would go over the narrow cliff into the lake.

Volcano interrupted honeymoon tranquility.

We breathed a sigh of relief when we passed through the difficult area and went on 18 miles south along the lake to the town of Bubondana. Fortunately, we reached a government rest house, a small unfurnished, mud-thatched building, and we took refuge there. We received the startling news that there had been 19 earthquakes that day. We stayed there a couple of days and then returned to our honeymoon haven because we learned that the volcano had erupted out of the side of the mountain and the lava mass was moving slowly. So now, jokingly, we say our married life began on a volcano and it has been erupting ever since!

Up until that time, this volcano turned out to be one of the longest-flowing in history and it continued for two full years. A year later we revisited the area and found that the mission station was completely burned out. The molten lava had devastated the virgin forest. It had flowed steadily into Lake Kivu and had sent up massive columns of steam.

As darkness came upon us the river of fire flowed brightly and an African pastor, who had come with us on this occasion, was so amazed at the sight that he said, "When I get back to Oicha station (where he was pastor) I am going into the forest and tell my brother, who does not know the Lord, that 'hell is a reality'! "

Jennie's Side of the Story

God had worked in a wonderful way to bring Jen into a knowledge of Himself and in His providence He worked out the plan that brought us together. This is the way Jen said it happened:

I remember well, at the age of 17, while walking on the sidewalk of my hometown in Northampton, Pennsylvania, how with self-satisfaction I enumerated all my accomplishments: I could drive a car, I had a job in the office at the Atlas Portland Cement Co., I taught a Sunday School class, and I could dance. I had arrived!

About a year later, my father, who was the superintendent of a Celanese mill, transferred to New London, Connecticut, and I moved along with the family. A neighbor girl, Ann Wistrand, who really knew and loved the Lord, invited my mother and me to a Bible class. "A Bible class?" I had never heard of a Bible class, but since she invited us we went. The class was held in the YMCA and taught by James Bennett, a lawyer from New York City who came to New London each week on business. I had never heard that kind of teaching before. It wasn't just relating historical facts, it was personalized and it related to me. He gave one illustration that clarified what Jesus had done for me. A farmer had a lamb that died. About the same time a mother sheep also died, so he thought he would bring the lamb left by the dead sheep over to nurse from the mother that had lost her own little lamb. However, the mother would have nothing to do with this lamb; it was not hers. The farmer skinned the dead lamb and placed the skin over the live lamb and took it again to the mother sheep. This time she smelled her baby and allowed the lamb to nurse.

He explained that this is a picture of what Christ has done for us. We sinners have no acceptance by a Holy God, but when we receive Jesus as our Savior, His righteousness covers us. As we come covered by His righteousness, we then are a sweet savor to God and fully accepted by Him.

Ann also invited us to attend a small Baptist church. With the nourishment I received through the Bible study and the instruction from the Word at the Montauk Avenue Baptist Church, I came into a knowledge of God's great salvation. I accepted Christ as my Savior and Lord and was baptized.

Up to this time, however, I knew practically nothing about missions and I don't remember ever having heard a missionary speak. One Wednesday night at prayer meeting, Pastor Ferguson showed slides on Africa. He read the script since no missionary was present, but it was that night that something happened in my heart. On the way home, it seemed as though my mother also sensed this for she said, "Would you like to be a missionary?" I don't recall what I said, but I do remember how surprised I was that she should ask me because during those days, we didn't talk about spiritual matters. We were of the staid opinion that such things are very private.

Several years of inward struggles and "growing pains" followed. I was working in the office of the Robert Gair Company and had quite a responsible position. However, from time to time, the Lord, through many various circumstances, reminded me of His call to go to Africa. My fears and lack of commitment made for further delays, until one day I remember so specifically that the Lord said to me (not in an audible voice, but it might as well have been because it came so forcefully to me, as if He were speaking), "If you don't go now, I won't bother you again."

I thought, "How terrible if I miss out on what the Lord really wants me to do." I told Him that if He would give me the courage, I would do what needed to be done. I would tell my father, leave my work, and go to Bible School to prepare. I didn't tell my father I was going to go to Africa, only that I was going to Bible School. It was hard for him to understand why I would leave a good job and go to Bible School. Later, when I told him I was going to go to Africa, this shook him even more but, praise the Lord, eventually he understood and was glad. When I told my boss at work, he left me for a short time and then came back and offered me a substantial raise if I would stay. He asked me to think it over. The next day I told him, "No. I will be leaving." The day I left, he took me into the office of the plant superintendent and told him I was leaving that day and he said, "I even used the devil's weapon to entice her to stay but it didn't work."

During my years at Montauk Avenue Baptist Church, Florence Young discipled me and actually got me involved in many outreach activities. She organized a Saturday morning children's meeting and had me give the Bible lesson. She gathered the young people for a Friday night Bible study and had me teach. On Sunday afternoons we taught Sunday School classes at Lake's Pond Church in Waterford. Florence was also helpful as I searched to know how to become a missionary. When she heard that Mrs. Wentworth, a missionary from Africa, was going to speak at the Huntington Street Baptist Church, she suggested that we go and hear her. She also learned that Dorothy Shipman had come home from Kentucky, where she had been serving as a missionary, and suggested that we go and visit her to get some ideas relative to missionary work. On another occasion a group of young people from Providence Bible Institute were going to be at the Waterford Baptist church so she said, "Let's go and hear them." We did, and this proved to be a part of the Lord's plan.

The Church asked me to be Superintendent of the Junior Department of the Sunday School and I served in that position for several years. During the summer I initiated and conducted the Vacation Bible School at both the Montauk Avenue Baptist Church and Lake's Pond Church. I joined the few who, once a month, held a meeting in a nursing home and occasionally brought the message.

My studies at Providence Bible Institute, 1933-36, enabled me to grow in my knowledge of the Word of God and prepared me to communicate His truth better to others. In my third and final year at Bible School, fear got the best of me and I got the bright idea that there was a needy area there in New London in which I could work. I told the Lord all about that need and that I would be happy to serve there; however, I never did feel at peace about this. One day, Dean Smith announced that Doris Groat, a graduate of the school, was returning from her term in Africa and would be speaking at Chapel the next day. Since I had no peace about my own proposal concerning my future ministry, I prayed earnestly that the Lord would really show me what He wanted me to do and that if He really wanted me to go to Africa, Doris herself would approach me. Well, the next day Doris spoke in Chapel and on the way out she caught up with me and said, "I understand you are interested in Africa. I would like you to come up to my room after lunch. I would like to talk to you." From then on there was never a doubt in my mind, the Lord did want me to go to Africa.

I applied to the Africa Inland Mission and was accepted. On March 1, 1937, with a memorable send-off by family, relatives, church and office friends, I set sail on a freighter, the *West Cawthon*, with a party of 12 A.I.M.ers, 8 missionaries and 4 children. There was a lot of waving as we pulled away from the dock. The last I saw of my dear mom was her waving good-bye to me.

The Lord called her Home just a little over three years later. How I grieved because all my plans to tell her about these many new experiences were shattered. That same year Sid's mother also went to Glory so we were a comfort to each other. We spent one month going from New York to Cape Town and one month up the east coast of Africa to Mombasa, Kenya. Then we three single girls drove inland, arriving at Aba, Belgian Congo (now Zaire) three weeks later, a distance of approximately 15 hundred miles.

Shortly before leaving for Africa, my cousin up on the farm in Pennsylvania said, "If she's going to Africa, she needs a gun!" He gave me a 30-30 rifle and taught me how to use it. He put a tin can on a post up on one of those beautiful rolling hills of Pennsylvania and taught me how to shoot. Well, I practiced and practiced, and would you believe it, I got so good that one of the first things I did when I got to Africa was to bag a deer: no, not a deer, a d-e-a-r—Sid!

At this writing, we celebrate 56 years of married life together. I thank the Lord for the way He has led. It gets "good-er and good-er" all the time. We make decisions all through life, but I am grateful that He enabled me to make that greatest of all decisions, to receive

Newlyweds.

Christ as my Savior and Lord. The proof of His Lordship was tested when He gave me that call to go to Africa. In faithfulness He granted His enabling and He has fulfilled His promise, "Lo, I am with you alway" (Mt. 28:20c).

Chapter 6

Blending Our Lives and Ministry

Jen and I were now entering into a new era. Two had become one and the Lord gradually blended our lives together. How did this take place? We had our own quiet times of communion with the Lord and from the very start we had daily prayer and the reading of the Word together. We soon learned that the closer we drew to Him, the closer we drew to each other. With Joshua we prayed, "...as for me and my house, we will serve the Lord" (Josh. 24:15c). We wanted the Carpenter's Son to be the constructor of our house for, "Except the Lord build the house, they labour in vain that build it..." (Ps. 127:1a).

We became partners in each other's ministries. It was wonderful to have Jen as part of our evangelistic safari team. She was able to make this part of her schedule during the school vacation months when the girls returned to their villages. This added a new dimension

Home sweet home—Aba.

to the "bush" ministry. Her presence was a delight to the women and girls as they had someone to whom they could relate. We trekked over the narrow African paths from village to village, living among the people and setting up our camping gear in a grass-roofed village hut. We loved it. This was home away from home. We visited every household and witnessed to everyone. Meetings were held in the chapel, if they had one, and out under the trees if they didn't. Jen reveled in sessions with the children and they sang the Bangala choruses with gusto. African pastors traveled with us and gave the cultural touch in messages spiced with vivid African illustrations that captivated the hearts of the audience.

Living with the people enabled us to feel the pulse of African village life. We learned of their joys and laughed with them. We learned their sorrows and wept with them. They had a deeply ingrained fear of the spirit world, which, they said, could bring sickness and death as well as devastation and destruction to their gardens. Epidemics spread rapidly through vast areas and took their toll. Without village medical help available, they appealed to their witch doctors who, for a fee of a goat or a chicken, went through traditional rituals to appease the angered spirits. We came upon many who had heavy hearts. We shared the Word of God with them and pointed them to the One who is able to meet all their needs. We are grateful that many responded and were set free from the bondage of the past and became a living reality of the truth, for "If the Son...make[s] you free, ye shall be free indeed" (Jn. 8:36).

Jennie with pygmies by banana leaves hut.

Life in the bush was far from dull. Each day contained new experiences, and it was marvelous to see the Lord lead. On one occasion, we were enroute to the town of Watsa, about one hundred miles from our station, and we decided to make an unplanned stopover in the village of a Paramount Chief where there was no testimony. Some of the people were resistant to the gospel, but the chief was very warm and he gave us a hearty welcome. As a result of our friendly relations with him, he invited us to speak to all the people in his large village. He encouraged the people to come; and there was a large crowd. What an opportunity! No doubt most of them knew very little or nothing at all of the gospel. They listened intently as we unfolded the greatest story ever told. Pastor Muse Wuli, who was with us on this occasion, had such a good rapport with the chief that he was asked to come and live among them and minister to the chief's people. At a later date, Muse established his home there and was blessed in his ministry.

Equator at 9,030 feet.

While residing there, Muse decided to penetrate the government gold-mining camps that employed thousands of African workers. He was challenged by the tremendous need in so many camps that were without a church or school. He sought and received government permission to begin a work at Camp Bumva, and the response among the people was exciting. As a result of Muse's outreach, five camps were opened and served by pastor-evangelists. The mining officials looked with favor upon the work that was being done and opened the door for missionaries to enter this restricted mining area. In the years that followed, we had many opportunities and thrilling experiences of preaching every night in the different camps. God blessed with much fruit and vibrant churches were established. Many of the Belgian supervisors were so impressed that, from time to time, they invited us into their homes. Through these opportunities to witness, strong friendships developed.

Ed Schuit, one of my warm-hearted colleagues, and I went on a safari into the Kilo-Moto gold mining area to minister to the hundreds of workmen and their families. When we arrived at Camp Bumva, we were invited to stay in the home of Monsieur Godan, the Mining Supervisor. Pastor Muse Wuli, who had planted the church in this camp, had also been used of the Lord to bring Monsieur Godan into a knowledge of Christ and had nurtured him in the Lord. We used his home as a base for an expanded outreach in several surrounding camps. This afforded us an opportunity to have fellowship with him. He had worked for the government mining company for many years and had many interesting experiences.

One story that he told really impressed me. On one occasion the Belgian Mining Syndicate decided to celebrate the success of their years of labor and invited the mining engineers from all over the country to meet together for several days in one of the large cities of the Congo. High government officials and mining executives

Ed Schuit and Sid studying by lamplight in mud hut.

On safari.

Table in the wilderness.

and their wives all were on hand. On the last evening of their celebration, a sumptuous banquet was prepared, numerous speeches were made, and the festivities of the evening were climaxed by the presentation of a beautiful diamond to a lady of very high esteem. It was in the form of a necklace and was placed around her neck. She expressed her gratitude in rather profuse terms, as only French-speaking people can. She removed the necklace to gaze upon the beauty of the large diamond and decided to pass it around so that all the guests could see it. As it was passed from person to person, such exclamations could be heard as "beautiful," "gorgeous," "exquisite," etc. No doubt every adjective in the French language was used.

Finally it came into the hands of an old man, who had been a prospector during the early days when Africa was known as the white man's grave. When he received the diamond, he handled it very gently, took out a magnifying glass, placed it in his eye, and began to scrutinize the costly gem. Some time passed and he made no exclamation. His expression was one of deep concentration and thought. Everyone wondered at the actions of the old man. Finally, the lady who had received the diamond became very curious and could wait no longer. Calling the old man by name, she said, "Monsieur, do you see any defect in that diamond in that you gaze upon it so long and make no comment?"

The old man did not respond immediately, and after a period of strained silence he began to speak. Still not lifting his eyes from the stone, he said, "No madam, I do not see any defect in this diamond; it is one of the most beautiful I have ever seen. But, Madam, I do see something in this diamond. Would you like to know what I see?"

She quickly responded, "Yes, Monsieur, I would like to know just what you do see in the diamond."

After another moment of silence he began to speak slowly and said, "Madam, I see blood, the blood of men who died from malaria, blackwater fever, dysentery, and the plagues of Africa in order that such a beautiful diamond as this might be produced."

As I pondered this, I was reminded of the fact that there are trophies of God's grace the world over. Their testimonies are rich; their lives are fragrant and fruitful. They shine and glitter in the background of heathenism all because the Son of Righteousness doth dwell within their hearts. We know that first of all they are diamonds of the grace of God, made such by the blood of the Lord Jesus. But we might say that in those diamonds we see the blood of multitudes of the Lord's servants who have laid down their lives for the cause of Christ; those who have been cut down in cold blood or have succumbed to the plagues of Africa. Their blood is the seed of the Christian Church. Ah, yes, there is blood in those diamonds!

This was evidenced in the ministry of Miss Lucy McCord. Lucy was a radiant, humble Irish lady who had gone to the Congo in the early 1920's. She and her sister worked as teachers among the people of the Logo tribe at Todro station. Her sister died of malaria after a few years on the field, and about 20 years later Lucy came down with a serious case of bacillary dysentery that played havoc with a previous condition she had of pernicious anemia. She was brought to Aba hospital, and Dr. Kleinschmidt did all he possibly could for her, but she continued to get worse. One day doctor sent word to all the missionaries on the station that he didn't expect Miss McCord to live more than a few more hours, and he invited us to gather to bid her farewell.

Never will I forget that scene. About ten of us stood in a semicircle about her bed. We sang hymns that bespoke the glories of Heaven and various Scripture verses were quoted at random. "Let not your heart be troubled...In my Father's house are many dwelling places...I go to prepare a place for you...that where I am, you may be also" (Jn. 14:1-3 NAS). "I have fought a good fight, I have finished my course, I have kept the faith: Henceforth there is laid up for me a crown of righteousness..." (2 Tim. 4:7-8) "There remaineth therefore a rest to the people of God" (Heb. 4:9).

Then each of us went in turn to the bedside and gave Miss McCord a final word of comfort and encouragement, which was followed by a closing prayer, committing her to the Lord. We all were very conscious of the Lord's presence and our hearts were strangely moved as we returned to our homes. A few hours later she slipped on to Glory.

The next morning we gathered for the funeral service at the station cemetery. A large crowd of the Logo tribe people who had known and loved her were on hand. Missionaries spoke at the graveside and many outstanding things were said concerning her ministry. But the most stirring eulogy was given by Pastor Matayo Varayo, the Logo Pastor from Todro station. Filled with emotion, he began to speak with quivering lips, *"Madamo Lucy azi mama na ngai sopo na Mokonzi."* (Miss Lucy is my mother in the Lord.)

He had come out of a heathen village as a young lad and had gone to school at Todro where he was taught by Miss Lucy. She had led him to Christ, nurtured him, and watched him grow spiritually. She encouraged him to go on to Bible School and then he served as a pastor in the bush for many years. At a later date he was chosen to be the pastor of the large station church and God had blessed him. He certainly could say, "Miss Lucy is my mother in the Lord." Ah, yes, there is blood in those diamonds!

Bush Bible conferences were held at the end of each month in a different region. They were joyous occasions. All the plans were made well in advance and the Christians planted large gardens to provide food for the occasion. Temporary grass shelters were built to house the scores of guests who came from distant places. These gatherings had spiritual depth to them because they were bathed in prayer and prayer was a vital part of the program. Messages were given by African pastors and missionaries. Singing by choral groups and the congregation with the accompaniment of several trumpeters was always a high point in the conference. Fellowship around the Word in this fashion was a real stimulus and encouragement as well as being a challenge to a greater commitment to the Lord. Many unbelievers who attended responded by accepting Christ. The final gathering was held at night around several large bonfires under the starry heavens. It was really a hymn-fest interspersed with thrilling testimonies glorifying the Lord. These mountain-top experiences prepared them for the conflicts they would experience in the valley. Thank God, He is not only the God of the hills but also the God of the valleys (see 1 Kings 20:28).

It was this kind of a conference that Jen and I attended at our chapel on the high hill overlooking the town of Watsa. Circumstances that arose there taught us that missionaries always have to be flexible. The Christians built a small grass shelter that was to be our home for the next few days and it adequately took care of our needs. The roof was covered with fresh-cut long African grass. The size of the hut was just large enough for our two cots with an aisle between. We fit in very comfortably and really enjoyed our camping setup.

One night, when we were tucked in our beds and safely under the protection of our mosquito nets, we settled in for what we thought was a good night's sleep after a long and active day. However, the rumbling of thunder in the distance announced an approaching storm. When it reached us it was a full-fledged tropical downpour accompanied by wind and lightning. In a short period of time, the rain poured through the grass roof like a shower bath and rivers of water came down the hillside and ran through our humble dwelling. It felt like we were at sea and the boat had sprung a massive leak! I got up quickly, slushed through the water, got a tarpaulin out of my car, and (with the help of our concerned African brethren) put it over the entire roof. Sleeping was a little damp but finally the rumbling of the storm moved off into the distance and all became quiet. It was all part of a day's safari.

One of our regional conferences took us into the Kaliko tribe, located about 80 miles from Aba. The people in the numerous local villages had responded to the gospel, and most of them had pastor-teachers who were zealous for the Lord and worked harmoniously together. The Bible conferences they arranged from time

Pastors Muse, Yakobo, and Yokana.

to time were stimulating and challenging. It was an encouragement to see the growth that had taken place.

The churches in that area always went out of their way to make us feel welcome. They had prepared well for our coming. On our arrival, crowds were there to greet us with hearty and prolonged handshakes. We knew that we were wanted. To really make us feel at home, they had thoroughly cleaned one of their mud and thatched dwellings. As we entered the hut, we were amazed to find that they had papered all the walls with the pages of a Montgomery-Ward catalogue! This was "royal treatment." They sought to make us feel comfortable in our own cultural setting. We expressed our gratitude for their thoughtfulness and all the work that was involved, for they had pasted the pages to the wall with manioc root flour paste. Evidently it had been decorated that very day before we arrived. However, that night when we got comfortably settled in our mosquito netted cots, lo and behold, we began to hear a tearing of paper. "Mickey mice" came out of their hiding places to feast on the wall paper paste! They literally tore up the place in a wild frenzy. All through the night we heard the rattling of paper being torn from the wall. By dawn all the paper was in shreds on the floor! This was one of the unplanned-for sessions in the Bible conference schedule that had to do with "men and mice," and a good time was had by all—even the mice.

Christmas is always a high point in the life of the church in Africa. Christians and non-christians alike looked forward to it. They came in to the station from 75 village churches scattered as far as 100 miles away. It was the crowning station conference of the year. Much preparation was necessary as there would be between three thousand and four thousand on hand for the occasion. Everyone participated by bringing food. Shelters for sleeping quarters had to be built and firewood collected, as well as large amounts of water carried.

Two days before Christmas, people came from every direction: men, women with babies on their backs, young people, and school children. Most traveled by foot, others by bicycle or by getting a ride on a truck. They sang hymns as they traveled and arrived in high spirits. They were jubilant as they met friends whom they had not seen for a long time.

The day before Christmas was highlighted with various games and competitive sports. Many of the Greek merchants entered into the spirit of the occasion and contributed all sorts of garments that were used as prizes. The fun time concluded with a spirited soccer game. In the evening, they partook of a sumptuous meal, enjoyed jovial chatter, and then sang hymns on into the night.

Early Christmas morning, while it was still dark, a group of carolers stealthily came to our home and awakened us with the sound of "Joy to the World, the Lord is Come" and several other beautiful carols. Then all our family went out to greet them. It was very picturesque as they stood there under the starry heavens with the pastor leading them in the light of a small kerosene lantern. Following our greetings, the pastor prayed, thanking God for His unspeakable gift. Then, following the "Amen," the crowd all shouted "Merry Christmas" in English. Our family responded accordingly and we expressed our sincere gratitude to them for coming to our home. Then they continued on to all the missionaries' homes. It was a heart-warming experience.

Christmas Day was the high day of the "feast." The church was packed to overflowing with several thousand on hand, all of whom were dressed in their best clothes. The colorful garments and bandanas of the women and girls were exotic and beautiful. The congregation responded to the energetic song leader with the accompaniment of the large old-time church pump organ and the blaring of trumpets and trombones. It was a thrill to join them as they harmonized with "Hark, the Herald Angels Sing, Glory to the newborn King," "Silent Night, Holy Night," etc. One could not help but ponder all that God had done to bring a great crowd like this out of the spiritual darkness of pagan religious traditions, bowing down before their stick-like gods, now to worship the true and living God, the babe of Bethlehem's manger! Such is the transforming power of the gospel. Numerous choirs added their melodious voices in adoration of the Savior who had been born to redeem those from every tongue, tribe, and nation. A powerful message was given by the African pastor, telling of the miraculous birth, life, death, and resurrection of our Lord. When the invitation was given to accept the provision God had made for their salvation, many responded and Christ was born within their hearts. The service lasted at least three hours, but there was rapt attention and no one thought about time.

Following the meeting, there was a great feast and everyone was fed *ugali* made of cassava flour, cornmush, rice, and fresh buffalo meat. The African women had prepared all this in 50-gallon drums that had been cut in half, making wonderful cooking pots for the occasion. You can be sure their mouths drooled and tummies were filled.

In a wonderful way God had made provision for the meat, which is always considered the important part of the meal. Many of our Africans had old "muzzle-loader" rifles, the type that were used back in the 1800's. A month before the conference, I had given several cans of gunpowder to our African hunters in hope they would get all the meat that was needed. However, due to an extended rainy season, the bushland grass had grown quite high and had not been burned off, which made hunting difficult. Thus, all their efforts had been fruitless. This was a cause for concern. The day before all the guests were to arrive for the conference, I decided to go out with several hunters. Starting at 5:30 a.m., we drove about 30 miles to an area where we previously had been successful in getting bush-buck and waterbuck. By faith we pulled a half-ton trailer along to bring home the "bacon!" Many had been praying that the Lord would feed the several thousand as He did at Galilee. As we trekked into the bush, we could see that we were in for difficulty. The grass was still six to ten feet high and we literally had to break our way through this jungle. After several fruitless, disappointing hours, in the heat of the dry season with the sun now high overhead, the time for good hunting was past. So, we decided to return to the car and I can assure you, it was with heavy hearts. Then suddenly we were startled by a thrashing sound in the bush and a huge buffalo came into view with its rear end facing us. That was not a good posture for a shot, but under the circumstances we had no other choice but to shoot. The huge beast turned and began running broadside through the tall grass, which prevented getting a good aim. Nevertheless, I took the best aim I could, as it was moving with great speed, and fired. But to my dismay, it continued to run on into the bush. I thought that I had missed and felt too exhausted to run after it, so I handed my rifle to one of the African hunters, hoping he could get another shot. To my surprise, within seconds he came back with the word that it was dead. The random shot had pierced its heart. This happened just about 11:30 a.m. Back at Aba the missionaries had gathered for their daily prayer meeting and prayed that if it was the Lord's will, we would get meat. God granted the request of all who prayed and brought great joy to more than three thousand who were fed.

Chapter 7

Building the Church

In 1964 the Muslim government of Sudan ordered the expulsion of all the missionaries in the southern part of the country. The last two of our Africa Inland Mission missionaries to leave were Gerry Rineer and Don Fonseca. When they bade farewell to Pastor Andarea Vuni, it was a scene charged with emotion. As they tearfully embraced each other, Anderea said, "We are sorry to see you go, but do not fear for us; the Church is here. If it were your church or our church, we would fear; but it is Christ's Church, it is God's work. It will not die, it will live." This is true of the Church of Christ throughout Africa, especially in areas where it has gone through the birth pangs of political turmoil. It has not succumbed; it is vibrantly alive, thus fulfilling the promise of our Lord: "I will build My church; and the gates of hell shall not prevail against it" (Mt. 16:18b).

The Africa Inland Church, in each of our fields, was born as a result of the prayer and the dedication of the

**Part of Aba station.
Church in center.**

early pioneers who followed in the footsteps of our founder Peter Cameron Scott. They sought to penetrate areas and unreached people. They were men and women who knew God and were strong in faith. Having laid their all on the altar, they did great exploits. Like the apostle Paul, they determined to know nothing among them save Jesus Christ, and Him crucified (see 1 Cor. 2:2). They endeavored to become an integral part of the lives of the people to whom God had sent them. They did this both linguistically and culturally, becoming all things to all men that by all means they might win some. They preached the simple gospel, illuminated with African illustrations. They were confronted with great odds and opposition by the religious traditions of the tribes. But the Spirit of God broke through centuries of spiritual darkness, opening the eyes of a few individuals who were nurtured with prayer and the Word of the Lord. Miracles took place as they did in the early New Testament Church, and the infant church emerged and grew to approximately two million baptized believers. The reason for this was the faithful proclamation and teaching of the Word of God, which was translated into the language of the people. It was given line upon line and precept upon precept, as in the days of Nehemiah. "They read from the Book...making it clear and giving the meaning so that the people could understand what was being read" (Neh. 8:8 NIV).

Trumpeters at evangelistic meeting.

With the expansion of the church into new areas, it was soon realized that trained leadership was essential. Therefore, Bible schools were started to prepare faithful men who would be able to teach others. As time passed, further growth took place. Bible colleges, seminaries, and graduate schools came into being, meeting the needs of advanced theological students. Theological Education by Extension (TEE) was developed to prepare many laymen who, because of family responsibilities, were unable to attend the colleges. Commensurate with the goals of the Africa Inland Church, the A.I.C.

Missionary College is now preparing experienced pastors to plant churches among remote unreached tribes.

David Langford teaching seminary class.

The church at Aba station was a part of this planting and growing process, and God blessed the efforts of outstanding missionaries who launched the work. I had the privilege of being one of those who followed in their train.

In 1939 Roy and Kitty Brill went home on furlough and I was assigned the position of station superintendent. This greatly increased my responsibilities. Beside all the maintenance and building work, and the supervision of over one hundred workmen, my greatest joy was the giving forth of the Word and working with the pastors and evangelists. Together we sought to give leadership to the church.

It was a delight to meet regularly with the pastors and elders as I had much to learn from them. We sought the Lord in earnest intercession for His guidance in matters of evangelistic thrusts, disciplining new believers and those who had fallen into sin, establishing

Aba church council.

Christian standards, and dealing with cultural conflicts that were contrary to Scripture.

Up to this time, Aba church did not have an ordained pastor and, therefore, it was my responsibility to function as chairman of the elders' meetings, to perform baptisms, to minister the Lord's Supper, to perform weddings, etc. After attending a number of these sessions, I had the strong feeling that the national church leaders, who were men of God, should have the positions of authority, and I told them I thought they should choose one of their number to be prepared for ordination.

It was a great day when this actually happened and Pastor Muse Mude was ordained before a packed-out church. He was a very humble man and theologically prepared. For a number of years he had served in the "bush" and then as leader of Aba Station Church; now the time had come for this special recognition. Following his ordination I told him that he was now the *Motu na Kiti* (chairperson) in our elders' meetings and that he would perform the baptisms and serve the Lord's Table. He said he wanted me to assist with the baptisms, but I thought it wiser to have him perform them. He did insist that periodically I should administer communion and share the pulpit.

For many years Sunday services were held in the auditorium of the boys' school building, which accommodated about three hundred. Two services were held, and the overflow sat on benches on the wide veranda. This forced us to consider the need for larger facilities. A committee discussed the construction design, and I drew up the proposed plans. Together, with the church leaders, we went over the plans and the cost of construction. Fortunately, a fund of twenty thousand dollars had accrued and was available for the work.

The job of putting up a building 115 by 43 feet was a major task. Tons of rock had to be transported to lay the foundation, and about two hundred thousand bricks and thousands of Roman tile had to be made. Large trees needed to be felled and sawn according to specifications for the roof. The work was launched in prayer, and day by day we looked to the Lord for His wisdom and guidance as we labored with the workmen. It was a challenge to all of us, and there was a real spirit of camaraderie among all those involved in the construction because this was to be a house of worship to the One who had given His all for us.

The erection of this sanctuary was very similar to the gigantic task of planting and building the Church of Christ in Africa. It could also be compared with the challenge that was given to Nehemiah, namely, the rebuilding of the wall about the city of Jerusalem (Neh. 2:17–6:15).

Nehemiah was stirred when God revealed the tremendous need to him. The wall of the holy city had been

Gathering for church service.

destroyed by the Babylonians. This was judgment from God because of the sins of the children of Israel. The prophets of the Lord had foretold this and of their captivity that would last for 70 years. Following this revelation, God moved and melted the heart of Nehemiah, who in deep contrition confessed the sins of Israel. He prayed and God answered miraculously, calling him to rebuild the wall (Neh. 1–2).

God revealed the devastating spiritual needs of the people of Africa. He burdened and broke the hearts of those who were to be early pioneers of the Africa Inland Mission. He answered their fervent prayers by calling them to go forth to plant and build the Church of Christ in Central and East Africa. Like Nehemiah and his compatriots, they and their colleagues said, "Let us rise up and build."

However, it was not without determined opposition from their adversaries. The missionaries soon realized that the enemy would contest every advance they endeavored to make into his territory. "For we wrestle not against flesh and blood, but against principalities, against powers, against the rulers of the darkness of this world, against spiritual wickedness in high places" (Eph. 6:12). In the midst of the enemy's onslaughts, we are exhorted to "stand." We stand not in the energy of the flesh, but in the power of the Spirit and clothed with His armor.

God gave the organizational and management skills to Nehemiah and to the early missionary leaders. They knew that the desired results could be accomplished only through a cooperative effort. Therefore, Nehemiah enlisted the skills of each of the tribes of Israel. They had various abilities and came from different social backgrounds. They were assigned their tasks and worked shoulder to shoulder (see Neh. 3). What an example for national and missionary builders of the Church of Christ today, that those from every tongue, tribe, nation, and various strata of life should be working shoulder to shoulder and hand in hand. There are those who will put their "necks to the work" wholeheartedly, and others who will not. But the work goes on, just as it did in Nehemiah's day.

The missionary soon realizes that he is in the midst of a battle and, like Nehemiah, the battle lines are drawn (Neh. 4). Prayer is essential, and those involved are both builders and warriors. They have a trowel in one hand and a sword in the other. In the midst of the conflict, the missionaries and the nationals carry on the building of the Church of Christ in the same way. In one hand they had the trowel of ministry as an evangelist, pastor, theologian, doctor, nurse, teacher, pilot, engineer, etc. In the other hand they have the Sword of the Spirit, the Word of God. Together, both hands are dedicated to the Lord of the Harvest for the building of His Church. As with Nehemiah, it is God who strengthens their hands for the work and it is God who enables His servants to complete the task triumphantly (Neh. 6:9,15).

The policy of the Africa Inland Mission, ever since its inception in 1895, has been one of progressive evangelism in every phase of our ministry for the purpose of planting churches and equipping African Christians for positions of leadership. The result has been encouraging. Some planted, others watered, "but God gave the increase" (1 Cor. 3:6b).

Our goal has been to work ourselves out of a job and to give complete autonomy to the Africa Inland Church. It began by training local Christians in theological schools. These men later became ordained pastors of station or bush churches, which were made up of various ethnic groups who resided in the area. Each station church elected elders who, with the pastor, made up the local supervisory council. As growth took place, regional councils were formed with representation from each local church, and they in turn appointed those who would represent them on the Administrative Board of the Africa Inland Church. Various committees, chosen by the Board, were responsible to the Board for the different departments of the work. This was the general organizational pattern that was carried out in countries where the A.I.C. and A.I.M. served.

Mission leadership, working in close cooperation with the national leaders, produced significant maturity in each group, preparing them for the ominous clouds of change appearing on the horizon. The continent of Africa was restless during the 1950's. African leaders were emerging to challenge the rights of colonialists to rule their land. Like fires burning over the African plains in the dry season, the fever of independence spread wildly over the continent. *"Uhuru"* (freedom) was on everyone's lips. The violent struggle that took place brought tremendous political pressure and demands upon the African church. It became a time of transition for both the church and the mission. Wise mission leaders became aware of the church's dilemma and saw the need to adjust to the new circumstances. Innumerable consultations were held and it was a time of much prayer, seeking the will of God.

Although the circumstances were different in each country, the Africans rightly sought and were granted complete autonomy. In some areas the transition went comparatively smoothly, while in others it was only after much sympathetic and cooperative discussion together that we arrived at our goal. For some missionaries the adjustment was hard. Still others were convinced that the "scaffolding of the mission" must come down, so that the church could be seen standing as the work of God in an African context. In actuality, it was the greatest hour in the mission's long history. Like the early Church, which was forced out of Jerusalem by persecution in order to fulfill God's purposes, the A.I.M. was pressured by circumstances to acknowledge that its leadership role now must change and submit to the authority of the church which it had brought into existence. The African church was now in the driver's seat of the new organization, but it wanted the missionary alongside to help apply the brakes if he saw danger ahead. Second Corinthians 1:24 expressed the new status of the mission and its missionaries as it relates to the church: "Not for that we have dominion over your faith, but are helpers of your joy." It became clear that the mission's image must be reduced. We were now under the jurisdiction of the Africa Inland Church and it was in control.

Properties held by the mission were relinquished, and missionaries were now to be approved and assigned by the church. Mission Field Councils became Field Committees caring only for missionary affairs. Field Directors became Field Secretaries. When agreements were finally concluded and the dust of the turbulent decade of the 60's had settled, a new era of mission history had dawned.

The church now emerged carrying great responsibilities, and of necessity a relational change took place between the mission and the church. The celebration held at Machakos, Kenya, in October 1971, was in many respects, what took place in all our major fields (of course with many variations). The A.I.C. wanted to establish a definite date for the transfer of authority to take place. Twenty thousand Christians came for the occasion from all over Kenya. Mission leaders and government officials participated, including the Vice President at that time, Daniel Arap Moi. The program was interspersed with a great fanfare of bands, choirs, and numerous speakers, all packed into the four-hour ceremony. The mission officially gave full autonomy to the church in this impressive manner, and missionaries committed themselves to serve as partners with the church. It was a historic milestone.

I counted it one of the high points of my missionary career to be asked by the church to speak on behalf of the mission. I spoke from Second Timothy 4 and likened the scene there to the aged Paul coming down the final stretch saying, "I have fought a good fight, I have finished my course," as he passed the baton of responsibility to Timothy, his son in the faith., I emphasized the tremendous charge that Paul gave to Timothy. I likened this scene to a one-mile indoor race that took place in the Melrose Games in Madison Square Garden in New York City. Erik Barnett, Kenya Field leader, and I went to see that race because Kieno Kipchoge, an outstanding runner from Kenya, who was also a member of the

**Historical meeting—
Africa Inland Church, Kenya, became autonomous.**

Africa Inland Church, was one of the contestants. Because of our love for Africa, we wanted to cheer him on. When the time came for the one-mile race, participants from all over the world were lined up. The starting gun

WORLD
RECORD
HOLDER

KIPCHOGE KEINO

**Kipchoge Keino
(American Tract Society).**

was fired and off they went. To our dismay, Kieno stayed behind the pack and remained in the rear lap after lap. Our hearts sank. Each time he passed by we would shout as loudly as we could, "Come on, Kieno," and tried to cheer him on. But there was seemingly little change in his pace until it came to the last few laps. When Kieno began to step out and surge forward, we were thrilled and we shouted louder to encourage him. Then he moved out ahead of all the runners and, sprinting at a fast pace, finished about fifteen feet ahead of the one who came in second. This was a cause for excitement and great joy because his victory was also our victory.

I explained to the great crowd gathered for the occasion, "This is an illustration of what is actually happening today. The Africa Inland Mission, like the apostle Paul, is handing the baton of responsibility to its son in the faith, the Africa Inland Church, and the charges given by Paul to Timothy are applicable to the church family." I said to them, "If you lag behind in the Christian race we will grieve. If you fall by the wayside our hearts will be broken. We will agonize in fervent prayer and supplication that you will '...lay aside every weight, and the sin which doth so easily beset us, and...run with patience the race that is set before us, looking unto Jesus...' [Heb. 12:1-2]. If the church does this, it will finish its course victoriously and with exceedingly great joy, and your victory will be our victory and cause for overflowing rejoicing and praise to God."

I reminded them of the great national event that took place on December 12, 1963, the day that Kenya received its independence from the British government. Several hundred thousand gathered in Nairobi stadium for the occasion. Before that multitude Kenya's first president, Jomo Kenyatta, received the baton of government responsibility that was passed on to him by the Prince Consort, who represented the Queen. It was done with dignity, great pomp, and ceremony. In President Kenyatta's acceptance speech, he recognized the solemnity of the hour. It was the birth of a nation, which was finally realized after years of political turbulence. He knew the dawn of a new day was taking place because of the united effort of the people. The president, aware of the enormity of his task, urged all to assist him in the building of the nation. To emphasize that fact, as he concluded his message, he shouted over the vast amplification system, *"Harambee."* It was a Kiswahili word understood by everyone, exhorting them to strenuously and harmoniously work together. The massive crowd agreed by responding in unison, *"Harambee."* The president repeated this three times and the people answered accordingly. It was a thrilling moment.

On that memorable day at Machokos, when the baton of responsibility was handed over to the national church leaders, I felt constrained to conclude my message before that large crowd of Christians and missionaries by exhorting them with that same Kiswahili word. I shouted over the amplification system, *"Harambee,"* and they all responded with *"Harambee."* I did this three times and they responded each time. We all knew that, with the help of the Lord, we must work and strive together, putting our hearts and hands to the task of building the Church of Jesus Christ.

Today the Africa Inland Church, in all of our fields, consists of approximately two million baptized believers who are involved in about seven thousand churches, nurtured by some five thousand pastors, and the work continues to grow under national leadership. For all that has transpired we say, "To God be the glory; great things *He* hath done."

Times of change are good times to reevaluate goals and objectives. Though relationships and structures may have changed, the mission's objectives remain the same. We are mindful that so much more needs to be accomplished to meet the challenge of unreached people groups who echo the Macedonian call to the mission and the Church of Christ throughout the world. It is a plea that is constantly repeated by the African church leaders: "Come over and help us" (Acts 16:9c).

Chapter 8

A Desert Place

It was the height of the dry season in Sudan and there had been no rain for a period of three months. Nearly all the rivers and streams had dried up. The lack of water presents real problems for the villagers and is especially burdensome for the women who are responsible for the daily water supply. It is a familiar scene to see the tribal women laboriously digging down into a sandy, dried-up riverbed until they strike a small trickle of water that gradually seeps into the pit. They dip out the contents with their gourds and fill their water pots. It is a long, drawn-out process under the blazing 120° heat of the tropical sun. As the dry season progresses, they must go deeper and deeper to reach the precious supply. They dread the day when there will be no more because everyone will have to find another source, which may be miles away.

As one flies over the massive geographical expanse of Sudan, the largest country in Africa, he is amazed at the vast desolation of the land. Even though old Mother

Digging for water in dried-up riverbed.

Nile, with its mighty flow of water, wends its way northward in a serpentine fashion through the center of this sun-baked country, the river produces only a narrow ribbon of green vegetation on either side. The vegetation is abruptly cut off by the dry soil a short distance from its banks. The words of the concerned disciples to the Lord Jesus while He was ministering to the five thousand, "This is a desert place" (Mt. 14:15), describes the Sudan very realistically.

Sudan borders the northeastern corner of Zaire, and the many missionaries assigned to that area traveled by Nile steamer, which slowly plodded its way a thousand miles southward through the Nile sudd to the town of Juba, the capital of Equatoria Province. Juba was the seat of the British Colonial government and a commercial center. It had a variety of small shops run by Arab, Greek, and Egyptian merchants. Occasionally we drove the 135 miles from Aba in the Congo to stock up on special provisions.

This gave us contact with many friends of the Church Missionary Society. These folks were very warm and totally dedicated to the Lord and to the proclamation of the gospel. The almost boundless area of equatorial province was their responsibility. It was because of the Christian fellowship our missionaries had with them that their leader, Archdeacon Gibson, invited the A.I.M. to consider working in the Sudan.

**Pioneers
John and Mabel Buyse.**

John Buyse, one of our pioneer missionaries, had numerous contacts with our British friends and showed a keen interest in the tremendous need that existed in Sudan. As a former sailor on a Dutch sailing vessel, he was always viewing new horizons. As a result of his mother's prayers, he had accepted Christ by the helm of the ship and asked Jesus to become the pilot of his life.

His burden for the Sudan grew as he learned of 17 unreached tribes on the east bank of the Nile. The Anglicans of C.M.S. had partially penetrated the area, but they lacked personnel. In their contact with John Buyse, they felt constrained to explore the possibility of challenging the A.I.M. to take over the responsibility of that great expanse east of the Nile up to the Ethiopian border. Following numerous meetings with leaders of

the Church Missionary Society and government officials, the challenge was accepted in 1948. This was in
answer to the fervent prayers of John Buyse. He immediately made plans to return to the United States to en-
list the support of the Home Council and to obtain
missionaries for this new thrust. During that time, the
Congo Field Council (which also had been involved in
all the negotiations) was invited by Archdeacon Gibson
and the Sudan government to send a survey team to investigate the possibility of establishing a work among
the Latuka tribe living on the Lopit Mountain range.

Plans were arranged by George Van Dusen, the
Congo Field Director. I was invited to accompany him,
together with Dr. Ted Williams and Roy Brill. To me,
this was a challenging spiritual adventure. With all our

**Carlton Booth, Ralph Davis, George VanDusen,
Howard Ferrin studying map with Archdeacon and
Mrs. Gibson.**

camping gear packed in a half-ton trailer attached to my car, we started off for the city of Juba. Arriving there, we conferred with Archdeacon Gibson and then drove another 80 miles to the small town of Torit. This was a military base for the Southern Sudan Defense Force. We were hosted by British army officers, and the next day we met the Latuka Paramount Chief, Loturo, who was to be our guide. He ruled over the thousands who lived on the Lopit Mountain range, which was about 50 miles long. He was very friendly. He did not know English, but that was not a problem because we had an excellent C.M.S. Sudanese pastor and he was our translator.

It was the month of February and very hot. The road we traveled was rough and rocky and could be used only in the dry season. The rocks and boulders made it very treacherous, but with much prayer it was negotiated without damaging the vital underparts of the car. It was about 5:00 p.m. when we arrived at the chief's village. Their conical grass-roofed huts and cattle corrals were high up on the sides of the mountain, which rose to six thousand feet. We set up our camp in the foothills alongside of what was supposed to be the road. It was good to relax after an arduous journey. Although weary in body, we were in high spirits, no doubt similar to how Joshua and Caleb must have felt spying out the promised land. They said, "...Let us go up at once, and possess it..."; "...The land is an exceeding good land. If the Lord delight in us, then He will bring us into this land..." (Num. 13:30; 14:7-8).

Early the next morning we were greeted by Chief Loturo and about 200 or more of his people, elders of the tribe, and young warriors, all unclothed. The women and the girls wore animal skins and there were many children. They chatted away in the Latuka language, making many remarks about their foreign visitors. They were inquisitive to hear what we had to say. The chief told them of our arrival and they, no doubt, had talked about us around their fires the night before. They were all friendly and sat as a group on the ground, awaiting our message.

The fact that these people were without the gospel was foremost in our minds and presented a tremendous opportunity. The chief introduced us to his people and then we had the privilege to tell them about those things that were upon our hearts. The only way we could communicate with them was through a double interpretation. We spoke in English and the Sudanese pastor translated it into Arabic and Chief Loturo gave it in Latuka. We expressed our gratitude for the privilege of being with them and then we asked a question, "Do you believe in God?"

They said, "Yes, we believe in God who has created the heavens and earth, the trees and vegetation, domestic and wild animals, and the grain we plant. We believe in God. He is a good God, but we do not worship Him. It is the spirit world that we worship, as the spirits of our departed ancestors may be angry with us and cause sickness and death and the destruction of our crops; therefore, we have to appease them by worshiping them with our sacrifices and offerings."

We continued by asking them if they had ever heard of Jesus and what He had done for them. They responded, "How can we know what Jesus has done for us as we do not have a book to tell us about Him?"

They saw us standing there with open Bibles in our hands and they reminded us that they didn't have such a book as we had. This was a humbling reality that shocked us. It placed the blame at our feet. It made us aware of the fact that this was indeed a "desert place." The rivers of "living waters" had not flowed through this land. Therefore, it was a thrill and it gave us great joy to tell them, in simple illustrative terms, the "good news" and why Jesus had come. They listened intently to these strange new words. They had never heard these words before, and they were very different from the word of their forefathers. We told them that we wanted to come and live among them, to teach their children in school, and to establish a hospital that would care for their physical needs. The chief led his people in discussion and together they gave their hearty approval. Our initial goal attained, we traveled with the chief about 30 miles further along the north side of the mountain to Logotok, a lovely spot in the foothills, which was chosen for a station site. This was to become a gospel lighthouse, piercing the darkness, and a "fountain of life" in a desert place for one hundred sixty thousand Latuka tribesmen.

This trip into the Sudan opened my eyes and heart to the overwhelming spiritual needs of the multitudes among 17 unreached tribes. They were the "other sheep" (Jn. 10:16a) that our Lord said He must also bring. I would have volunteered immediately to join the Sudan team, but I felt this might be too presumptuous. Therefore, I committed the whole matter to the Lord to work out His perfect will.

In 1949 John and Mabel Buyse led the first group of A.I.M. missionaries into the Sudan, including Bill and

Dorothy Beatty, Betty Wilson, and Olive Rawn. A short time later they were joined by Barbara Battye and Martha Hughell. Their base of operation was Opari station among the Acholi and Madi tribes. Within a year they expanded to Katire Ayom and then up to Logotok among the Latukas. Schools and medical work were started. Dr. Douglas and Kim Reitsma gave supervision to the latter on each of the fledgling stations. A hospital was established at Logotok where they were joined by Barbara and Martha, and later on by Dallas and Winnie Green and Henry Senff.

The early days of the A.I.M.'s Sudan advance was a time of roughing it. Nearly everyone lived in mud and wattle, grass-roofed houses. The members of the team worked well together and put themselves to the task of learning the Acholi and Latuka languages. The schools thrived with eager students and the medical work drew many to the hospital and station dispensaries. They accepted every opportunity as a channel to present the gospel.

In 1952, just before we went on furlough, our family visited the Sudan. We wanted to see the work and to learn all that was happening so that we could stir hearts in the homeland. During our visit, Uncle John, as everyone called John Buyse, approached me about the possibility of taking over his responsibilities as Field Director. He was in his early seventies and felt that someone else should be taking over the leadership. I told him that I was greatly challenged by the tremendous need and that I would have volunteered for work in the Sudan following the survey trip a couple years before, but I had thought that might be too presumptuous. Therefore I had placed it in the hands of the Lord.

I said that if this was the will of the Lord, I would be happy to come, but I wanted to be sure I was moving according to the will of God. Uncle John was a godly man, a man of prayer whom I greatly respected. We concluded our time together by getting down on our knees beside his bed and committing the whole matter to the Lord of the Harvest.

While on furlough, I learned that John Buyse had written to the U.S. Council, suggesting that I be appointed for the task. After consultation, I was given this new assignment. This was to be a big change for Jen and me and the family. We looked to the Lord for His enabling and sought to urge our friends and churches in the homeland to undergird us with their prayers.

During that furlough period, Dr. Ralph Davis, the U.S. Director, received an urgent message from John Buyse about a crisis situation that arose. It concerned a government order stating that we had to have a good all-year-round supply of water on each of our stations in order to continue with our boarding schools. Dr. Davis informed me of this serious dilemma and said there was a New York businessman who was interested in meeting this need but he wanted to know all the facts. He asked Dr. Jim Propst and me to meet him in his office. I had slides of the work that portrayed the need, and Dr. Jim, besides being a medical doctor, was also experienced as a water engineer. It was our privilege to meet with a Mr. Frazer in New York. He was warm and understanding and wanted full information. As a result of our presentation, he gave ten thousand dollars for the project. Immediately we searched for a used well-drilling rig, and one was located that was already mounted on a truck. We drove it to Philadelphia and spent about a month preparing it for shipment.

Earl Dix, one of our experienced missionaries from Zaire and a gifted multiple engineer in practically any type of mechanical work, met the shipment on its arrival in Mombasa, Kenya. After putting it all together, he and his wife, Helena, drove it toward the Sudan. Earl had never drilled a bore hole in his life; so

Drilling for water.

while en route, he decided to spend a week at Craelius Drilling Company in Uganda to learn some pertinent pointers to assist him in this new adventure. He had personal contact with the Swedish workmen and told them of the task he was about to tackle. This resulted in one of the experienced drillers accompanying him to provide some practical on-the-job instruction. This proved invaluable, and then Earl continued on his own and successfully completed wells at our five mission sites.

It was just at this time, in 1953, that Jen and I returned to the Sudan to take up our new assignment. We were based at Katire Ayom, which was back in the bush among the Acholi tribe. The first drilling took place here. It was thrilling to see all the people gather around the newly installed hand pump to dedicate the well to the Lord. This took place during the height of the dry season when water was so difficult to find, making it extra meaningful to the people.

The British Government officials were so amazed at the way Earl Dix had successfully accomplished the task that they asked him if he would drill some wells for the government. He agreed to do so because this would pay for the cost of all the Mission wells. Up to this time, as far as I know, no such project had been carried out in Equatoria Province, and the success of this additional phase of the operation gave us a good rapport with the government and the people.

The Latuka village of Labalwa was one of the places chosen by the government to be explored for water. It was located about six miles outside of the town of Torit. During the five months of dry season, the Latuka women walked this distance during the cooler hours of the morning to get their daily supply of water from the one river. The river became a small creek then, flowing down from the Imatong mountains and through the town of Torit. It was a time for the women to relax and bathe. Then, around four o'clock in the afternoon, they would make their way back, trudging those six miles carrying two five gallon tins of water, one on top of the other, on their heads with babies on their backs. As we watched this scene day by day, our hearts and backs ached for them.

One hot, dry-season, day Earl Dix arrived with the drilling rig at the village of Labalwa. Excitement ran high among the more than two hundred residents, but there was also some questioning as to whether water really would be found. As Earl surveyed possible drilling sites, he came to the conclusion that the most logical spot was between the only two large trees on the fringe of the village. An audience of young men, who were the *Muni Minji* or "warriors" of the tribe and therefore spoke with a measure of authority, exclaimed that no water would be found in that spot. They had been there for years and knew the area and spoke with an air of positiveness. They even laughed at the ignorance of making such a choice. Nevertheless, Earl continued to set up the rig and start drilling. All went well until he struck rock and then the progress was much slower. The large six-inch drills had to be heated in a charcoal fire until they were glowing red and then Earl sledge-hammered them to the proper size and sharpened them. It was hard work and had to be done repeatedly.

After four days of drilling, the first supply of water was struck. We discovered this when the long tubular bailer was lowered down into the bore-hole to clean out the well, and when it was brought to the surface it was filled with water. When the valve was released, water gushed out all over the place. The tall lanky Latukas dove for the water and began taking a bath. Dogs, goats, and chickens, all went after their portion of the precious liquid. Following a couple more days of drilling, a tremendous amount of water was struck, and Earl wanted everyone in the village to experience the joy of what the Lord had done. He told them to bring all their pots, pans, buckets, and drums and he would fill them with water.

We planned for this to take place on a Sunday afternoon and to make it an evangelistic thrust. Our missionaries from Logotok station, who knew the Latuka language, were all on hand. Jen and I brought a truckload of our Christians from the town church in Torit. It was a gala occasion with jubilant singing. The villagers arrived with every water container that could be found in the village.

What a sight to see this large crowd seated on the ground around the drilling rig, patiently waiting to hear what we were going to say. Nationals and missionaries spoke, emphasizing the message Jesus gave to the Samaritan woman at the well when He said in John 4, "Whosoever drinketh of this water shall thirst again: But whosoever drinketh of the water that I shall give him shall never thirst; but the water that I shall give him shall be in him a well of water springing up into everlasting life" (Jn. 4:13-14). "...Jesus stood and cried, saying, If any man thirst, let him come unto Me, and drink" (Jn. 7:37b). "...Let him that heareth say, Come.

And let him that is athirst come. And whosoever will, let him take of the water of life freely" (Rev. 22:17).

We sought to make the message contextually relevant to the great need they experienced every day during the dry season. Water from an earthly source was needed for physical life, but could only quench their thirst and meet their need temporarily. We had come to tell them of heavenly springs and rivers of living water that flowed from Calvary, which would cleanse them of their sins and fully satisfy the thirst and deep desires of their hearts for time and eternity.

At the end of our message, one withered old man said he had something he would like to say. He stood up and gave a short history of the village, saying that for years they had great difficulty getting water in the dry season and because of the laborious task of carrying it a great distance, it had been hard for them to get other Latuka clans to give their daughters in marriage to their sons. But now, with the discovery of water in this new well, it would change the course of their history. Then he went on to say, "When I die, I am going to tell all those who have died before me that all down through the years there was hidden water right beneath our village."

We could not help but follow through with a comment on the words of this village patriarch by saying, "When we came to your village to start drilling, you laughed at us saying, 'There is no water down there.' " But we drilled and came upon this tremendous supply of water. The water down there was hidden from you all these years. We have come to tell you of other waters that God has provided for you, but which have been hidden from you and your people down through the centuries. We repeated the message of the gospel, exhorting them with the words of Isaiah, "Ho, everyone that thirsteth, come ye to the waters..." (Is. 55:1) and of the Psalmist, "O taste and see that the Lord is good: blessed is the man that trusteth in Him" (Ps. 34:8).

It was a joyous day for all the people of Labalwa's and a triumphant day for each of us, especially for Earl and Helena Dix. They saw the fruit of their labors as they filled every receptacle in the entire village with life-giving water. As we began to leave, a group of the young boys of the village returned to Logotok with our missionaries to enter school.

We retired that night with our cups full and running over with thanksgiving to the Lord.

Chapter 9

Desert Storm

Winds of change have blown all over Africa, from hurricane and tornado strength in some areas to gentle or gusty breezes in others. Sudan experienced all of them. Stormy gales roughed the expansive desert, forming wave-like dunes and clouds of sand flying high into the heavens, blurring the sun. Fine gritty residue found its way into every household in Khartoum, the capital city. The Arabs call it *haboob* or "sandstorm," and it depicts the history of this great country.

The Sudan started as a collection of small independent states. In 1820, the conquest by Egypt brought about their unification, but unfortunately it resulted in great exploitation and maladministration. At that time a Sudanese leader arose, proclaiming himself the Mahdi, or awaited religious leader. He started a revolt that brought about the fall of Khartoum in 1885, and as a result, he controlled Sudan for 13 years. This was followed by a reconquest by the Anglo-Egyptian forces in 1896, and a condominium government was formed in

1899. They ruled jointly until 1954. The Egyptians controlled the north, which was predominantly Muslim (fifteen million). The British administered the vast and sparsely populated southern area of seven million Nilotic and Bantu tribal groups, largely animistic and about ten percent Christian.

After more than 50 years of colonial rule, the pressures of the continental winds of change began to be felt and demands were made in the north for political change. Therefore, a plebiscite was taken to permit the people to make a choice for either British or Egyptian rule, or for complete independence. The overwhelmingly Muslim majority voted for independence. This caused great distress among the tribes of the south who feared Islamic oppression, which in the past had included a history of slave trading and suppression, causing strong animosity and division between the north and the south to this day. Therefore, they expressed their opposition by a show of force with thousands marching on the governor's office in Juba, armed with bows and arrows and spears, demanding that the British not leave the Sudan. It so happened that Jen and I had dinner with the governor and his wife that day and learned what was happening. The governor said he explained to them that the vote had been taken and the British government had to honor the decision of the people.

Missionaries began to feel the impact of the decision when Arab officials in the north replaced the British District Commissioners and the Provincial Governors. Mission leaders were called in for a conference with the new leadership, and we were told we would have to confine our ministries to our chapels. We would not be permitted to minister to the people in their villages. Medical work was terminated because they knew this was giving us a good rapport with the populace. Our doctor was expelled and the nurses were limited to caring for the physical needs of missionaries. All these restrictions were diplomatic moves for the purpose of stimulating our withdrawal, but we determined to stay on.

Although we meticulously avoided involvement in the politics of the country, we were told that they were suspicious of us. Even though we confined ourselves to preaching and teaching in our Torit chapel, occasionally northern soldiers could be seen walking around the outside of the building during our Sunday morning service. They listened for anything that might be construed as anti-government. Happily, restrictions were not put on our Christians concerning propagating the gospel in the villages, so we continued to carry on our work in spite of the obstacles. This was the beginning of the new government's plans to eventually remove the missionary threat to Islam.

Four months before the date set for independence, tension began to build up between the southerners and their northern leaders. This was felt in the town of Torit, which was a military base for the Southern Sudan Defense Force. The British had trained the Southern soldiers well. They were disciplined, and they highly respected their military officers. However, during the early days of the change of government and the transfer of power, the new northern officers were very apprehensive of the troops under their command. They feared rebellion and, therefore, didn't permit them to have their rifles. This made them feel that they were being dealt with subtly. They protested, saying that during the British regime they always carried their rifles.

Under pressure, the Muslim officers returned their guns, but without ammunition. The soldiers said they were not being treated fairly, so ammunition was issued to them; but when they discovered it was only sentry ammunition, they concluded that they were being tricked and this was the last straw. They kicked over the traces, raided the ammunition storage, and mutinied against their northern officers, killing 70 of them. One did escape in a truck and reported to his commanding officer in Juba what had happened. The general found himself in a difficult situation. He had a contingency of southern soldiers under his command. The soldiers were armed, and he feared when they learned what had happened in Torit, they too, would mutiny. Therefore, he felt he must disarm them.

In order to do so in a military fashion, he had both the southern and northern soldiers march separately out on the parade grounds as though it were a routine exercise. Then he called for the southerners to halt and come to attention. The northerners, who were a larger company, had no doubt been forewarned as to what was to take place. They were ordered to surround the southern forces. The southern soldiers were suspicious of what was taking place. The general then issued a command to the southerners, "Ground your arms." Hearing this, they were afraid they were going to be massacred. One soldier in the front line raised his rifle and aimed it at the general. The general hastily whipped out his revolver. They fired simultaneously at each other, and both dropped dead. A skirmish immediately took place. Some of the southerners fled, and others were subdued by the northern soldiers. This was the beginning of seventeen years of civil strife.

Torit was the official base of operations for A.I.M.'s Sudan field. It was where Jen and I resided and carried on the ministry of field leadership and also served the local church in various capacities. About two weeks before the mutiny, we decided to take a vacation at Rethy where our four children attended Rethy Academy in Congo (Zaire). We felt this would give us some extra time to be with them just before the end of the school term. What transpired from then on can only be explained as the miraculous providence of the Lord, who said, "I will instruct thee and teach thee in the way which thou shalt go: I will guide thee with mine eye" (Ps. 32:8). "...Lo, I am with you alway..." (Mt. 28:20).

Our vacation was completed on August 17th and Rethy Academy graduation exercises took place at 9:00 a.m., to enable the parents who had long distances to travel to get an early start. The program finished about 11:30 a.m. and then we began the process of packing the car. While in the midst of packing, a terrible cloudburst occurred. For about a half an hour we reluctantly stopped and sat in the car, wondering why the rain had to come at just that time. The roads would be slippery and we had to make the Pakwach ferry across the Nile River before it closed at 6:00 p.m. Uganda time, which was one hour ahead of Congo. Bill Beatty, my Sudan colleague, and I finally had our cars in readiness at about 1:00 p.m. We planned to travel together just in case we experienced any car trouble. A few miles outside the station, a huge tree had been cut down and lay across the road. The storm had scattered those who were working on its removal, but they soon returned to finish the task of sawing and moving the tree. Pressed for time, we wondered why this had to happen just now. As we continued, we found that many other trees had been blown across the road. We managed to drive around most of them, but one very large tree demanded some attention. An African hacked and we pulled. Finally other local help arrived, and the obstacle was removed. Fortunately, we made the Nile ferry and were poled across this fast-flowing expanse. This took us through the animal reserve where elephants, bush buck, and water buck came into view. Darkness overtook us as we climbed up the escarpment toward Nimuli. The motor began to sputter repeatedly, but then it would rectify itself for a short period. I wondered if I would have to stop to clean the gas filter, but we were able to continue on into the Sudan. Ordinarily, we would have continued our trip all the way to Torit (310 miles). We arrived at Opari station at 9:30 p.m. and still had 70 miles to go through a very sparsely populated area. In view of the problem we were having with the car, I decided that it would be wiser for the family to spend the night at Opari with John and Mabel Buyse.

Early the following morning I cleaned out the gas line and carburetor and we left after breakfast. As we traveled along, our children were discussing all the different things they were going to do during their holiday, and they played question-and-answer games. Mile after mile passed as we rode over the rough terrain and winding road. As we neared Torit, approximately eight miles from home, little did we know that an approaching army lorry of the Sudan Defense Force was going to change our plans for the next few weeks.

Armed Sudanese soldiers were not an unfamiliar sight to us, as Torit was the base for the Equatoria Corps. But being challenged to stop at gunpoint was something new. As we were drawing to a halt close to the lorry, we were scrutinized by its soldier occupants. When they saw that we were white people, they relaxed from their tenseness. I got out of the car and approached one of the "askaries" (soldiers) who had jumped to the ground. He briefly told me what had happened that morning in Torit and warned me to return to Opari as fighting was still going on in the town. He said it was very bad and that many of the northern Sudanese officers, government officials, and merchants had been killed.

Before turning the car around, we bowed in a word of prayer on behalf of our Torit pastor, his wife, and many of the Christians who attended our services. We then made our way toward another one of our mission stations, Katire Ayom. As we sped along we couldn't help but bless the name of the Lord for the cloudburst, the fallen trees, and a sputtering engine. These things irritated us the day before, but they were blessings in disguise. They made us decide to spend the previous night at Opari and prevented our family from being in the very thick of the fray in Torit.

During the last twenty miles of our trip to Katire Ayom the fuel tank registered "zero". With thanksgiving we pulled into the station. After making known the seriousness of the situation to our six missionaries there, we went to prayer for the Lord's guidance. "Happy is he that hath the God of Jacob for his help..."

(Ps. 146:5). "He shall call upon Me, and I will answer him: I will be with him in trouble; I will deliver him..." (Ps. 91:15).

After prayer we felt that all the women and children should prepare to leave for Congo early the next morning. Fortunately Bill had brought a drum of gas from Gulu. We did not ordinarily do this because we could always get a good supply from the Shell agent in Torit. We could see the hand of the Lord making this provision just at the very time we needed it. I tanked up and proceeded immediately to Opari to inform the Buyses of our decision, and our family spent the night there.

A short time after we had gone to bed, I heard a truck coming in our direction. I went out to the road to meet it to find out what the situation was in Torit. I shined the flashlight on my face so that they could see that I was a white man. The truck was loaded with armed soldiers and a Bren gun was mounted on the cab, ready for action. They were on their way to put up a military barrier at the Juba-Gulu-Opari intersection. They said things were very bad in Torit. When shooting began early that morning, it created a stampede among the civilian population, and everyone ran to the bush for shelter. Panic caused women and children to throw themselves into the swollen Kinyeti River in an effort to find refuge in the tall grass on the other side. Many who did not know how to swim were drowned. Others who found safety in the bush, later emerged from hiding to find that some of their children were missing. I was told that many of the northerners were killed immediately. Women and children were treated without mercy, but some were fortunate enough to escape into the bush or hide in buildings. The entire story was nauseating and made my heart ache.

Following this first skirmish, which had uprooted the inhabitants of Torit from the town and driven them into the bush, the soldiers became concerned for the safety of their families. When they found their wives and children, they loaded them on army trucks or any other vehicle and transported them out of the danger area. Thus began the stream of refugees. Most trucks carried twice their capacity. One half-ton truck must have had nearly three tons on it. The reports we got from the trucks that passed Opari on that first night were all the same—devastating.

Early the next morning (Friday) I had Dan Olsen transmit a message to the missionaries at Logotok station. They could listen in, but they did not have a transmitter. He told them about the uprising in Torit, advised them to sit tight, and said that I would try to get through to them sometime that day. That same morning I started off to Gulu in Uganda with my family and Mrs. Buyse. I thought that it would be wise for me to report to the District Commissioner since Great Britain was still represented in the Sudan government by the Governor General and was responsible to maintain law and order if all local efforts failed. Then too, by going ahead of the missionaries from Katire Ayom, I would be able to make arrangements for their temporary stay in Gulu. The District Commissioner was astounded at the news and immediately sent a telegram to the Governor of Uganda.

The following day we made plans for Dan Olsen to escort the cars carrying our ladies and children to the Congo, and we committed each other to the Lord. A cable was sent to the A.I.M. Home Office to inform them of what was taking place, and then Bill and I loaded three drums of gas and returned to the Sudan in his pickup. We carried a white flag that identified us as neutral. Each time we entered the Opari road we were challenged at gunpoint to stop. Soldiers armed with Bren guns and rifles hidden in the grass and behind trees halted our approach, but, when they saw who we were, they permitted us to pass.

When we arrived at Opari that evening, we learned that Enoka, our Torit pastor, and his wife had arrived safely. This made our hearts rejoice. They brought us the news that Dallas Green and his son Kenny had gone through Torit on his way to Juba early Thursday morning at 7:00 a.m., one hour before the conflict started. That meant Dallas was, no doubt, still in Juba, and that his wife, Winnie and his children and Barbara Battye were up at Logotok alone. We had been warned by the soldiers not to travel into Torit at night because there was too much random shooting. So Bill and I planned to try to get through to them the next day. However, while on our way from Opari to Katire Ayom, the lights of another car approached us. You can imagine our surprise and joy to find it was Barbara, Winnie, and the children. They had mistaken our radio message to say that the women and children were all being evacuated and thus thought they should leave immediately. We couldn't help but express our deep gratitude to the Lord for His loving watch-care over them. At that time Barbara did not have much experience driving in Africa, but she did a real good job. She confessed to being tired out, so I relieved her. Winnie said they did not have too much difficulty, other than being stuck in the mud on three occasions. Some Latuka warriors who appeared out of the bush at first seemed rather hostile but became friendly and helped to extricate them. Many times they were challenged by road sentries. Everyone, even the Latukas, assured them that the hostilities were not directed against Europeans.

After spending the night at Katire Ayom, I thought it was best for Bill to take Winnie and Barbara on to Gulu. I felt that I should go on to Torit to see whether our house and truck were still intact, and to try to obtain some policemen to guard the houses at Logotok. Winnie said they had only a couple of schoolboys watching the station. The Latukas have little conscience about stealing, and there was a possibility of the boys leaving and the houses being burglarized.

Noah Galla (a church elder) and I, traveling in the Greens' car with a white flag, which the soldiers had warned us to carry on the car, started on our way. The first military barrier was passed at Magwe without any difficulty. We learned that a northern merchant had been killed there. As we left Acholi tribal territory going into the Latuka area, the road took on a new appearance. Men, young and old, were heavily armed with spears. We passed numerous trucks, all loaded down with refugees. As we came onto the Torit-Juba road, a road sentry stopped us again. Torit, with its military base and large civilian quarters, was generally filled with activities of normal African town life, but now it seemed like a ghost town. Twenty or 30 dogs that had lost their masters had gathered together and were letting out high-pitched howls that sounded just like the death wail. It gave me an eerie feeling. The shops of the northern merchants had been looted, and papers were strewn over the ground. The few European shops had not been touched. Government buildings were closed up tight. All the prison inmates had been liberated as soon as the shooting started. Several hundred hospital patients had been vacated immediately. As I approached our house I was challenged by strongly-armed guards. I learned they were also guarding the airstrip by our house. As far as we could see, nothing within our wire fence enclosure was touched.

After getting my truck started, I had Noah take a guard, provided by the police, and go to Logotok. He returned with the good news that none of the mission buildings had been ransacked. Throughout the afternoon I heard occasional shots, but at 5:00 p.m. it sounded as though the whole artillery let loose right by our house. This continued off and on throughout the night. Red and green luminous flares would light up the whole area and then there would be bursts from Bren guns at an imaginary enemy.

Now I could understand why it was not safe to travel at night. It seemed as though the whole southern corps was on a manhunt. Their hearts were filled with bitter vengeance toward all northerners, not only for present grievances, but also for those of the past. They had stored these up in their memories for half a century, and their vengeance was running wild and taking its toll in lives. Many tribesmen have the proverbial "elephant's memory," especially when it comes to the Arab atrocities of 50 years ago. We were witnessing the birth pangs of a nation similar to those experienced in various countries of the world; history was repeating itself.

Sunday, the Lord's Day, was introduced by the blazing of guns. Ordinarily, it would have been a day of opportunity, ministering the Word to those who filled our chapel. The flock had dispersed to the four winds and the soldiers scattered throughout the town were tense with the expectancy of a clash with northern troops. They were keyed up to the point that they were ready to die in action. I set up my transmitter at 7:00 a.m. and hoped that I might be able to get a message through to the Sudan government in Juba or Khartoum. For three-quarters of an hour my signal went out without any response; then Bill Beatty came on the air from Katire Ayom and together we tried.

We learned later from Dallas Green, who was in Juba at the time, that he heard our transmission in Juba and informed the Sudan government officials that we were desirous of rendering whatever assistance we could in order to stop bloodshed, but there was no response. We did make contact with amateurs in Uganda and Congo; we informed them of the state of emergency that existed and asked them to contact authorities and, if possible, the Sudan government, to explain that security forces should be brought in immediately to stop further atrocities.

I learned from Noah that an Egyptian merchant and his wife and child had not been harmed and also that the Egyptian doctor was still alive. I was told then that they were all locked up in the merchant's house and would not come out for anyone. Noah said he feared that they lacked food and water. He also said that the soldiers wanted to kill the doctor. I wondered whether I could give any help to them, and after prayer I appealed to several of the southern soldiers who seemed to be in charge. I warned them that they should not touch any foreigners and asked if they would allow me to take the Egyptians to Gulu. When permission was granted, I went to see the Egyptians. I found that they had left their home and had gone to the Roman Catholic Mission about one mile out of Torit. They, of course, welcomed the opportunity to leave the area. So we arranged to leave about two o'clock that Sunday afternoon.

In the morning I spent much time trying to hide many of our household things up on the storage floor above the ceiling because I was sure that during our absence eventually someone would break in to steal what they wanted. There were many things that were impossible to hide. I felt that it was foolish for me to stay in Torit by myself. If the northerners captured the town and found me living alone, they might be suspicious of my presence. Throughout the morning I was desirous of preaching to the soldiers near our house, but the opportunity did not come until I was ready to leave. I called all of them together and gave them the gospel and then had a word of prayer.

When I went to pick up our refugee friends, I met the southern officer who was supposed to be in command. He said he had issued the order that shooting was to stop, but his soldiers were scattered over a hundred-mile radius so it was hard to tell when they would get the order and whether they would obey it, as every man appeared to be a law unto himself. My passengers consisted of two Egyptian couples and a child. The doctor declined to go. He feared that they might kill him while en route. The light brown color of their skin was somewhat similar to the northern Sudanese, and therefore there was a measure of danger attached to our travel. I also had a soldier and a policeman go along as escorts to enable us to get through military barriers. We had a word of prayer and committed our way to the Lord.

All went well until we were about 15 miles outside of Torit. Noah was driving my truck just ahead of me. We were brought to a stop by a southern road foreman. He told us that he had a northern merchant in his home and that the Latuka tribesmen wanted to spear him to death. Noah and I immediately rushed back to the mud and thatched-roof hut about 75 yards off the road. It was somewhat obscured by the tall kafir-corn garden and high grass. When we arrived on the scene, there were about ten naked Latukas surrounding the hut with their spears ready for action. Ordinarily one would speak somewhat meekly, seeing such an array of weapons and people with murder in their hearts, but I believe the Lord gave us holy boldness for the occasion and we sternly ordered the spearmen not to touch him. We told them of the cease-fire order that had been given by the officer-in-command and that we would take the merchant as a prisoner and hand him over to the British police authorities in Uganda. The Lord evidently prepared their hearts, for none of them went into action when we took the northerner, Mohammed Osman, back to the car and sped away from the scene.

I learned from the merchant, who was a humble man of about 35, that his shop had been looted; his mother, wife, and ten-year-old daughter, and two young nephews were mercilessly killed. He said they had tried to take his life five times. Once he was a prisoner in a room with a number of other northerners when the room was sprayed with Bren gun fire. Having escaped

Latuka warriors.

death, he was taken out to the airfield to be shot with ten others. As they fired, he ducked and ran for the bush. He spent several days without food and finally made his way to the house of the road foreman, who was a friend. The Latukas found out by some means that he was being harbored, and they determined to kill him. He pleaded with them not to spear him to death. He said he preferred to be shot and that they should have the soldiers on the next truck that came along to finish him off. In the Lord's providence, Noah and I were the next ones to come by.

We had a military barrier to go through before reaching our mission station at Katire Ayom. When we came to the road block at Magwe, we were halted by a crowd of soldiers and our car was scrutinized. We told them the cease-fire order had been given, but they didn't seem interested in giving heed to it and expressed hatred for all northerners. They could see that I had Egyptians in the car, but they were not concerned about them. In some marvelous way they didn't see that we had a northerner. When we were given clearance, we felt a lot easier, especially when we finally drove off and were on our way once again.

Bill Beatty had arrived back from Gulu where he had taken Winnie Green and Barbara Battye, and he was rather surprised to see the guests that I had brought along. The mission station was crowded with refugees, and soldiers seemed to be all over the place. The news soon spread abroad that we had a northerner with us. For safety that night we had some of our Christians posted as watchmen before and behind each of the houses. Bill and I slept in the same house with Mohammed Osman, just in case there should be any difficulty.

Mohammed Osmon and Egyptian family rescued.

Before retiring we gathered with our guests and read from the *Daily Light*, "I will instruct thee and teach thee in the way which thou shalt go: I will guide thee with mine eye" (Ps. 32:8). Then in prayer we committed ourselves to Him who neither slumbers nor sleeps.

The next morning the situation was tense. Numerous soldiers were in the vicinity of Bill's house where we were having breakfast. One made his way around the building again and again hoping to get a potshot at the northerner. The Africans who were working in Bill's house showed their concern so I went out,and after talking the matter over with Noah, we ordered all the soldiers to resort to the area where they were lodging.

Immediately following breakfast we prepared to get away as soon as possible. We all gathered for reading the Word and prayer, beseeching the Lord for His protecting hand. The Egyptian families got into the car without any difficulty, but it took some time to get Osman from the house to the car. I explained to him that we would have to make a pretense of handling him roughly. Many soldiers had congregated again and our Torit pastor Enoka came and whispered that some of the soldiers were talking about killing all of us because we were protecting this northerner. I called our soldier and police escort together and said that I wanted them to take the merchant by the hands as a prisoner and get in the car with him. We told the soldiers surrounding the car that we would hand him over to the Uganda police. Then, in a matter of seconds, we were on our way, praising the Lord for His undertaking.

Noah, a former military man, was well known by most of the soldiers; therefore, I had him proceed ahead, driving my truck loaded with his family and our Torit pastor's wife. Bill's pickup went next with a number of our African Christians. His car was well known to the military guards that we would have to pass because he had made several trips to Gulu, so I thought that it was wise for him to go second. The car I was driving was unfamiliar to the guards; therefore, I traveled last in our small convoy. The first military barrier we came to was at the juncture of the road on which we were traveling with the main Juba-Uganda road, about 30 miles from Katire Ayom. This area was heavily guarded. We approached this spot with a prayer for the Lord's enabling. I kept a little distance behind the other two vehicles to give them enough time to establish a friendly contact, and when I saw that they were not being held up, I increased my speed so that I could follow hard on Bill's tracks. The soldiers here knew who I was so I hung out the car window and waved and chatted with them as I moved on, trying to keep their attention off the passengers in the car. I was greatly relieved when we were waved on without being questioned. I said out loud, "Praise the Lord!"

As we turned to go south on the Nimuli road, Noah stopped the truck, no doubt to greet a friend; but I wondered why in the world he stopped at this particular place with all the soldiers right in the vicinity. I tried to get by him, even though there was a ditch on the side of the road. After maneuvering carefully around him, we started on our way. We had gone only about a hundred yards when an empty five-gallon kerosene tin that we had in our car expanded with a loud bang. I was sure we were being shot at and was greatly relieved when I learned what had happened.

Fortunately, there were no guards at the Nimuli border customs barrier. The police officials had left and the barrier gate was swinging in the breeze. Without difficulty and with much rejoicing of heart we crossed into Uganda. Five miles further on I stopped the car and we had prayer, thanking the Lord for His goodness to us. We continued on to the town of Atiak where we were met by a British military officer who, together with his troops, had been moved near to the Sudan border. I gave him a report of what had taken place and handed over our Egyptian friends and Mohammed Osman. Our prayers went with them, that through this experience they might be stirred to accept the Lord who had miraculously delivered them. I learned later that they had been taken to Kampala and then flown to Khartoum in Sudan. When they arrived there, the secular newspapers were stating that the situation in the south was caused by missionaries, but our friends informed the media, "If missionaries had not been there, no northerners would have been spared!"

Bill and I made our way back to Katire Ayom, where we stayed for about a month. Refugees continued to pour into the station and this gave us daily opportunities to give the gospel to an attentive audience. Finally, we heard by radio that northern troops had taken Torit. I feared for what might have happened to the Mission property and therefore decided to go there. I soon found out that my house and all the other homes had been ransacked. Fortunately, the thieves did not discover the things I had hidden above the ceiling.

Northerners who had been slain in the town were left on the spot where they had fallen. Vultures began to claim their prey until the bodies were picked up by truck, dumped into a massive grave, sprayed with gasoline, and burned. The first night after the northern troops finished the task of burying the ghastly remains, the hyenas let out hideous howls and yelps in protest at being cheated out of their feast of death. A lion, not ordinarily heard near the town, joined in the chorus with loud repetitious roars.

I stay on in Torit until the situation became relatively quiet and then returned to Katire Ayom. All during this time we had remained in contact with our Congo field, keeping them up-to-date on what was happening. Then Bill and I decided it was time for us to go to Rethy to begin the process of returning our missionaries. When we arrived there, we were given a jubilant welcome by all our "Sudan missionary family."

Four months after this, on January 1, 1956, Sudan received its independence. Great celebrations were held

in the north, but it was a different story in the south.
The people were very apprehensive. The mutineers had
been conquered and there was fear of being forcefully
suppressed by Arab officials who were now in charge.
Independence day in the town of Torit was a ceremonial
display of power since this was where the insurrection
had started. A large number of northern soldiers, ready
for any contingency, was on hand under the leadership
of the victorious general. The troops gave a display of
marching and drilling on the parade grounds. Then
they lined up for the final inspection and congenial approval of the former British District Commissioner, who
handed the baton of government responsibility to the
Commanding General. He climaxed the ceremony with
a strongly-worded speech that ended in a note of tri-
umph as the British and Egyptian flags were lowered
and the new Sudanese flag was raised high to the
shouts of the soldiers. They raised their rifles over their
heads and cried out in Arabic, "Shadit, Shadit, Shadit,"
implying, "We are strong and able to care for all the
needs of this land."

I wish I could say that the lessons learned from all
this led to tranquility and a stabilized government, but
that was not the case. Suspicion and hatred led to further bloodshed and civil strife for 17 years. Then a
shaky peace treaty was agreed upon in 1972. In the
midst of all this, "...God, who is rich in mercy..." preserved His church throughout the ravages of the desert
storm.

Chapter 10

Calm After Calamity

It was a day of rejoicing for our missionaries when they crossed the border back into the Sudan. We were grateful for the Lord's protection and conscious of the fact that He had gone before and opened the way for our return.

The political atmosphere remained tense for months, and the populace was apprehensive and fearful of retribution from the Arab officials and military leaders who were now in power.

Seventy-two northerners had been slain in the mutiny, and a military tribunal tried a number of southerners and found 72 of them guilty of atrocities. I was given the opportunity to speak to the first 12 who were sentenced to death. I prayed much about this awesome responsibility. Most of them were Latuka tribesmen who had little or no knowledge of the gospel. How could I make the message clear to them? I felt constrained to do it in a very simple and illustrative way by using the

Wordless Book and its black, red, white, and yellow pages. Each of the colors proclaims a corresponding message: Black portrays sin and God's judgment upon it, resulting in eternal death. Red reveals God's plan of redemption from the penalty of sin through the blood of Christ who died in our stead. White represents those who repent and accept God's provision of cleansing through the blood and receive forgiveness. Yellow speaks of the glories of heaven, God's village, where there is fullness of joy and pleasures forevermore.

Each prisoner was alone in a small cement cell that was about five by four by eight feet, with a small window opening near the top. A bucket in the corner was the latrine, and you can imagine the heat and stench when the door was shut. I spoke to each one individually, with an armed northern soldier standing guard and listening to everything I had to say. I spoke in Bangala and one of our church leaders translated it into Arabic. I urged them to accept the payment Jesus had made for their sins. Although 72 were found guilty, this was the only group I had the privilege of speaking to. Someone from another faith complained to the military that I was counselling his people.

Each morning at about 4:00 a.m. military trucks escorted those on death row off into the foothills of the Imatong Mountains where they were executed. Day after day this same procedure was followed. Whole Latuka villages in and around the town of Torit reverberated with the gruesome and mournful cry of the death wail, echoing shock waves of fear throughout the entire area. In view of the mutiny, the north felt they had to rule with an "iron hand." Under pressure, the south acquiesced and eventually time produced a surface healing, but underneath there were fires of resentment and hatred that exist to this day.

In spite of the political undercurrent and the uncertainty of the future, our missionaries carried on all the various phases of their work. The fact that we were there and sought to follow a familiar routine was an encouragement to the people and had a stabilizing effect on the community.

Translating Latuka New Testament
Martha Hughell, Barbara Battye and informant.

In spite of problems, Sudan is a land of challenge filled with opportunities for ministering to the spiritual needs of many tribes who are without the gospel. This included reaching out in a friendly way to the Muslim population who were not happy with our presence. The physical needs of the people also moved us with compassion, and our medical staff did as much as they could within our limited resources. Then there was always the surprise of the unexpected and the need to be flexible.

It was only a short time after we returned and were happily engaged in our work that another crisis arose. Late one afternoon Dan Olsen arrived in Torit and brought the shocking news that Bill Beatty had a paralysis that was spreading throughout his body. Olive Rawn, our efficient nurse, was fearful that it would hit his diaphragm and terminate his breathing. We packed hastily and made the two-hour trip over the back roads to Katire Ayom station.

In spite of the seriousness of the situation, Bill was calm. He could speak and his mind was clear. Dorothy, his wife, was naturally greatly concerned. Bill said he would like to be taken to Dr. Becker at Oicha Hospital in Zaire, which was approximately five hundred miles away. We made immediate preparation for the trip.

My car, a station wagon, was fixed up with a mattress. I carried Bill out, and Dorothy and Olive made sure he was comfortable. It was 11:00 p.m. by the time we left. We committed ourselves to the Lord to go before. Jen drove the ambulance car and I followed behind in Bill's pickup with a good supply of gasoline. In Uganda we encountered the aftermath of heavy rains that made the road very slippery. The curved crown of the road was so slick in one area that I had to push on one side of the car to keep it in the center of the road. Early in the morning we crossed the Nile river, at Laropi, on a pontoon. Then we came to a fork in the road. Both roads would take us to the Zaire border. We chose to take the shortest route, which was indicated on

a mileage sign. About 25 miles further on we came to a
river and the bridge was out. This was a disappointment. We learned from some of the Africans that a road
was in the process of being built that would connect
with the road we had chosen not to take. We decided to
see if we could make it over the rough rocky base that
had been laid down. I traveled ahead slowly until we
came to within 50 yards of the other road, but there
were no rocks laid over the black wet cotton soil. It was
impassable.

Pontoon crossing.

We decided to turn around and return to the forked
road and to continue our journey. The ambulance car
was back far enough so that it could turn around, and
they negotiated their way back to the beginning of the
rocky road. The truck was nearer the quagmire of cotton soil and in the process of turning around, one of the
wheels went down into the mud and became impossible

to extricate—"but God!" Just at that time I heard a truck coming on the main road; it was loaded with young men. I flagged it down and explained my plight, and they immediately came to my rescue. About 30 of them huddled around the truck and to the rhythm and chant of *harambee* (let us work together), they literally lifted the truck, foot by foot, out to the road. They were jubilant over the success of their labors and so was I.

With a grateful heart I was on my way, 25 miles back to the fork in the road and then 25 miles to the place where the ambulance car was still waiting. Bill had insisted that they wait until I was able to get to them. This delay hindered us from getting to the Zaire border at Mahagi until midnight. Negotiating immigration procedures at that hour would have been impossible, but when the African officials realized the seriousness of Bill's condition, they cooperated wholeheartedly.

As we went through the border (I was driving Bill's truck behind the station wagon), the lights from the truck revealed that gasoline was leaking from their gas tank. Evidently, it had been pierced on the rocky road. I smeared soap on the leak and was able to stop it. I filled their tank with gas and gave them an extra supply to take along, just in case I had any problem and became separated from them. I felt that they should continue to go on and not be concerned about my being able to keep up with them.

It was of the Lord we had made such arrangements. Around 1:30 a.m., just after we went through the small town of Djugu, a fire broke out under the hood of the truck. I immediately opened the hood and the flames shot out. Fortunately rains had saturated the sandy gravel by the side of the road. I hastily threw it all over the engine and put out the fire. Because it was dark, it was impossible to clean out the engine and get to the root of the problem.

The young African lad who worked for the Beatty's was travelling with me. Both of us slept in the cab until 5:00 a.m. when the dawn of morning light began to break through. Then I began the job of cleaning out all the sand and taping the wires that had been burned. I finally started up the car, but after going about a mile it began smoking. I knew that I could not go on and therefore returned to the town of Djugu where my Belgian friend, Francis, had an auto repair shop. While I slept, Francis worked on the car. The problem proved to be a stuck float in the carburetor. This spilled gas on a cracked manifold and caused the blaze. Gratefully, once again I was on my way and arrived at Oicha at 6:00 p.m. without further incident.

I was happy to learn that the station wagon carrying Bill had arrived at 10:00 a.m. after 35 hours on the road. Jen had driven all but two of those hours! After a thorough examination, Dr. Becker came to the conclusion that Bill's paralysis was caused by a strain of malaria that was found in the Sudan. In the providence of God, Bill eventually regained the use of his legs and the lower extremity of his arms. However, the shoulder muscles, controlling the movement of the upper part of his arms, were permanently impaired and never regained their full use. Following his recuperation, Bill returned to the Sudan and made a tremendous contribution to the work among the Acholi tribe. Through this entire experience I never heard Bill complain about what had happened, nor of his handicap. Instead, he doggedly sought to regain the use of his shoulder muscles by forcing himself to use them as much as he could.

Jen and I counted it a joy to work with our Sudan colleagues. They were dedicated to serve, in spite of obstacles and opposition. They were like many of those who rebuilt the wall of Jerusalem during Nehemiah's day, "the people had a mind to work" (Neh. 4:6c). Together with the national leaders, they laid the foundation of the Africa Inland Church in Sudan.

John Buyse pioneered the A.I.M.'s entrance into this land and set a fine example. He spent months up on the Lopit mountain range at Logotok putting up mud and waddle, grass-roofed housing and a hospital. At that time the government did not permit the construction of permanent buildings, so these were put up in preparation for the arrival of Dr. and Mrs. Douglas Reitsma, Barbara Battye, Martha Hughell, and Henry Senff, our first team to the Latuka tribe. The medical skills of the doctor soon gained the confidence of the people and became a wedge to open their hearts.

The culture of this animistic tribe was very interesting. They were a farming people and although they had cattle and goats, the raising of their crops took priority because this was their lifeline and existence. When the planting season started, they looked to their "rain maker" to provide this precious commodity. If the rains were delayed or if there was an unexpected drought, he was asked to petition the spirit world for their help. He, of course, expected to be reimbursed for his services with cattle, goats, chickens, etc. If the rains failed to come, they would have to bring more gifts. This was sometimes repeated again and again.

Family groups generally worked together, assisting each other in the digging of their gardens. Their blacksmithed, heart-shaped hoes were fitted as a spade onto a long pole. All the men would get down on their haunches and work together to the rhythm of an African work song, pushing their spear-like hoes into the earth ahead of them and turning over the soil. At the end of a long day they would celebrate with a feast of food or native beer.

Their cattle and goats were prized as their wealth. In a real sense they were their "bank account." They could be sold to obtain currency to purchase what was offered in the market place or as dowry for their wives. The size of their herds brought prestige and gave them status in the tribe. Therefore, cattle rustling became a way of life among them and resulted in palavers and tribal conflicts, which often ended in bloodshed.

Such a cattle-rustling skirmish broke out between two of the Latuka clans. A number were slain and many were wounded. One of these clans lived in close proximity to our hospital and was able to have their wounded cared for. But the other group resided some distance away and could not take their casualties to the hospital because it was in the area where their enemies were located. This would have meant another clash with them. The hospital, of course, was open to all, but the fact that one clan benefited and the other did not embittered the latter group.

During this time an epidemic of bacillary dysentery broke out and doctor was swamped with all sorts of cases. The presence of so many flies in the area carried the disease into the doctor's household. They not only became infected but evidently reinfected. They were not responding to treatment. As leader of the work, I felt that they should get out of the area for a temporary period of time until they were well enough to carry on their work.

During the absence of the doctor and his family, the clan (whose wounded could not be cared for at the hospital) thought this would be an ideal time to eliminate the medical service that was available to their enemies. So under the cover of darkness, they sent two of their warriors to the station to set fire to the grass roof of the doctor's home and the hospital. They did not touch any of the other buildings. Within a few hours' time, thousands of dollars' worth of equipment went up in smoke.

When the word reached me in Torit as to what had happened, I made my way out to the station early in the morning. I drove my truck along the rugged road at the base of the mountain. The mountain itself rose up to six thousand feet and the station of Logotok was in the foothills. As I came on the station, I saw the stark evidence of what had taken place the night before. The two buildings looked like skeletons draped in white ashes and my heart ached. A group of Latuka tribesmen were standing around and wondering what we were going to do.

There were two other missionaries on the station at the time. Together the three of us stepped into the still warm ashes of the doctor's home and gazed at the devastation. There was the doctor's library just a heap of ashes. The Scripture says, "In everything give thanks: for this is the will of God in Christ Jesus concerning you" (1 Thes. 5:18). So we decided to praise the Lord by singing the doxology together: "Praise God from whom all blessings flow...." Then we bowed our hearts in

Dr. Reitsma's home destroyed by fire.

Hospital destroyed by fire.

prayer, beseeching the Lord that He would use this seeming tragedy to His honor and glory and, if it pleased Him, He would even grant the "beauty for ashes" of which the prophet Isaiah spoke (Is. 61:3a). At a later date our request was granted when the government permitted us to put up brick buildings with metal roofs.

The loss of so much of their possessions and medical equipment was a shock and a keen disappointment to our two young medics. Nevertheless, they recognized it as an attack from the "enemy" and accepted it from the Lord as part of the cost of the offering they were called on to make when they laid their all on the altar of sacrifice. The mission family rallied around them, endeavoring to replace some of the things they lost, and doctors at other hospitals assisted them in getting reestablished by providing equipment and medications. Thus, they gradually got back into the full swing of their ministry.

In the midst of such difficulties, there was always a brighter side filled with joy and blessing. Such was the time when Joy Ritterhoff, Sanna Barlow (Rossi), and Ann Sheridan of Gospel Recordings arrived in Sudan to record the various tribal languages in our area. Joy and Sanna came to us in Torit, where there were numerous ethnic groups: just at that time we were in the process of getting settled into a building I had constructed and the ladies had to "rough it," but they were good sports and ready for anything. We were able to line up a number of nationals to be recorded. Most of them knew nothing or very little of the gospel.

This was our first experience of observing the technique used to record the message in a language unknown to the recordist. A translator who knew English and Arabic communicated with the individual being recorded. Sanna worked patiently through the whole process. One of the messages she wanted to get across was the parable of the lost sheep, with its challenging application. The translator asked the one who was being recorded to repeat the phrase given by Sanna in his tribal language. After this phrase was recorded, the next phrase was given and so on. They did this until the entire story was told of God's sending His Son Jesus as the good Shepherd, to seek and to save the sheep that was lost, thus making it applicable to all who would hear the message. The national who was being recorded phrase by phrase was not aware of the continuity of the message because he was only translating phrases. Upon completing the process, Sanna played back the entire story he had recorded and his reaction was amazing and fantastic. His response was "I never heard that story before." Some of our African Christians who observed the procedure were so thrilled at his reaction that they clapped their hands and ran about jubilantly rejoicing when they saw that the message had gotten through. Day after day this process was followed, recording various messages in numerous languages.

We thank God for Gospel Recordings and the impact they have made on all our fields. Literally hundreds of messages from the Word of God are listened to again and again in the people's own language, so much so that they memorize it and give it to others. Only eternity itself will reveal the fruit that has been produced.

In our effort to reach the masses of people in the town of Torit, including the Muslims, we were always seeking ways that might be used to reach out to them.

Up until this time, to my knowledge, movie film had not been shown in Torit. Since I had brought a projector to the field, I felt that this would be an opportune time to use it. The news was spread throughout the area and a large crowd came to the showing, which took place in the center of the town. Many from the Muslim community were on hand. The title of the film was "We Beheld His Glory," which presented the gospel in a clear and powerful way. Following the film we continued by showing Elsie Anna Woods' slides of her paintings on the life of Christ. They listened with intent interest. In view of the kind of the audience we had, I did not feel constrained to give an invitation. Only the Lord knows what was accomplished in their hearts. Our Christians were thrilled at the testimony given and it gave them further opportunity to converse with unbelieving fellow tribesmen.

Church services in Torit were generally packed wall to wall with people. Others stood by the wide-open windows on the outside and got more than "fringe benefits." It was a thrill to preach to them. Jen was excited about what was happening among the jubilant crowd of Sunday School children. Decisions for Christ were made in nearly all the services and we were encouraged to see the Lord work.

The zeal of our African pastors and lay leaders was used by the Lord in the development and growth of the work. Yosefa Mali was one who brought much joy to our hearts. He had received the Lord and had grown spiritually. He was very enthusiastic about helping Jen in the Sunday School. He listened intently to the flannelgraph lessons she gave each Sunday, then throughout the week he visited various villages and groups, using the same flannelgraph lesson. He became very excited about what the Lord was doing.

As time went on, he expressed the desire to go to Bible School in Congo (Zaire). (At that time we did not have a school in Sudan.) We were happy for this development, and he and his wife and family entered Adi Bible Institute, where Pete and Mary Lou Stam were in charge. It was a real step of faith to leave their own homeland and enter a school in another country and culture. Learning another language slowed Yosefa's progress, but he pressed on within his limitations with great determination. He was totally dedicated to the Lord and had wonderful fellowship with his classmates from various tribes.

Shortly after Jen and I had been assigned to the U.S. home staff, Mary Lou wrote to us concerning Yosefa and reported the following:

> Yosefa Mali and his wife, Elene, from Torit are here with us in the Evangelist School. Yosefa had language trouble for a while, but last January he showed considerable progress and especially in the last few months when he waxed bold enough to pray at our weekly prayer meetings. His prayers have been simple Bangala, but so sincere and sweet that we are sure that the Lord is well pleased. Two days ago he came up to tell me that his child, a twelve year old girl, was very ill. They had been treating her at the dispensary, but she had gotten worse and he was terribly worried. I jumped on my bike and went to see Danyele first [African infirmier in charge of the dispensary]. Danyele said that he could not find the girl's trouble and that he had made every possible test.

She was having kidney trouble and a low fever, but other than that he could find nothing. He suggested that I feed her milk to bring up her strength. I went down with an eggnog and found her breathing heavily and the dear parents standing around feeling so helpless. (Pete was at Field Council and David Richardson had not returned from Blukwa.) I prayed with them and I can still see that dear little mother as she held the child and said, *Nzambe azi* (God is, or He is able). I came away asking the Lord to give me such simple and yet such strong sweet faith in Him.

She took eggnogs regularly during the day and part of the next day. However, by Saturday morning she was worse and after talking with Danyele again we realized that she was dying. David had arrived from Blukwa and had offered to take her to Kuluva (A.I.M. hospital in Uganda), but Danyele strongly advised against moving her. He gave her all kinds of medication, but there was no improvement. Her breathing had increased in heaviness and she was suffering from such severe pain. The Lord took her Saturday afternoon at four o'clock. David and I went right down, and as we approached the doorway we saw the house was full and Yosefa himself was leading them all in prayer. He thanked the Lord for sending them to Adi, a land so far from their land of the Sudan. He thanked the Lord that his child, Yayi, was in the presence of the Lord. He thanked the Lord for this dear child who had been such a joy to them. "So great faith" coming from one who was born into a land that abounds in sin and heathenism. Elene was brokenhearted as she bent over the little form, but she, too, was so sweet with it all.

Most of the Bible School men prepared to dig the grave and have the burial that night, for they said it was so hard to have the body in the house all night and Yosefa and Elene had been up so many, many nights and they were worn out. What a blessing to see how those from so many tribes came to help. The sunset was glorious that night and we realized just a little of what that dear little child was enjoying at that moment.

They called us at 7:30 p.m. and said that they were ready for the service. Ruth Meredith, David Richardson, and I walked out to the grave. It was a beautiful moonlight night and we hardly needed a lantern. They quietly stood around the grave while Ezekele Ubimo led the singing. David gave a short message on *Kula bi na Nzambe* (The peace of God) from Hebrews 13. "That little grave will open again when the Lord will give Yayi a new body free from sin, stain, and all the matter of pain. *Nkembo atikali na Nzambe na mikolo, mikolo. Amina* (to God be the glory for ever and ever). Amen" was the way the message ended. They poured a small bottle of perfume over the body and then Yosefa and Elene each threw a handful of dirt in the grave. How our hearts went out to them, but their treasure was in heaven, safe in the Savior's keeping. Victory over the power of death and the grave! We thank the Lord for the privilege of proclaiming such a victory and for the privilege of training these men and women to proclaim that victory to others.

Mary Lou continued:

I was talking to Yosefa right after the burial right there at the grave. I asked him when Yayi had accepted the Lord and he said under Madamo Langford's teaching in Sunday School, June 1955 or 1956! He said she was such a joy to have around and she was such a help and he knew that she was truly born again. The teacher here at the Adi Sunday School said that she was very eagerly learning the verses from week to week. We broadcast the message to Rethy today and Sudan was listening in so they are praying for him.

I knew you would be interested to hear that, Jennie, and to know that your labor in the Lord was not in vain.

Chapter 11

Bringing Up Father

Following nine years of service in Congo, our first furlough was overdue. We had been held up by the ravages of World War II and now the time seemed opportune for our family of three- and one-half children to leave. As our missionary colleagues and national Christians bade us farewell, Mabel Gingrich said in her quaint drawl, "Well Sid, you're like Jacob; you came across Jordan with a staff in your hand and now you're going back with a multitude!"

Africans are very family-oriented. They are linked in a closely-knit intimacy, not only within their own households but also with all the members of their "extended family clan." Many times it is difficult to tell what their real relationship is to each other in the "clan." They refer to each other as *ndeko* (brother or sister), or they may speak of various older members as *ondo* (uncle) or as *mama* or *baba* (mother or father) or *tata* or *dede* (grandfather or grandmother). Whatever affects one member, affects all. They are *wedlocked together*—"in sickness and in health, for richer or for poorer, for better or for worse, till death do us part."

The presence of the missionary family creates a bonding relationship with African families and therefore presents a great responsibility and opportunity of testimony to both the Christian and non-Christian. The whole way of the missionary family life is naturally scrutinized. They allow for cultural differences, but we are all subject to the joys and sorrows of life and have similar feelings. Therefore, we relate to each other and there is a mutual concern for each other's needs.

As our children grew up, they enjoyed the wide open spaces of Africa. They loved to play together. They had

Langford family—Dave, Ginny, Lois, Ronnie.

their swings and a maypole. They climbed trees and their guardian angels, no doubt, worked overtime. When Lois reached the "playpen stage," she contented herself with dolls and toys. This took place on our wide screened-in veranda, which gave us the assurance that she was secure. We were reminded of the Lord's special protection when two baby puff adders, extremely poisonous snakes, were discovered under her mat.

Ronnie, our youngest, loved his two-wheel bike. As a five-year-old, he was delighted to exhibit his skill at riding and he handled it very well. One day tragedy struck as he went around a slight curve on the station road. The front wheel began to skid over some loose gravel and he went sprawling in a heap. In the fall the jagged edge of a broken plastic handle bar grip pierced his eye. Fortunately, I was at the house and had just finished our radio network schedule. He was unconscious and one of the African men carried him to me. The whole area of his eye lid was swollen and bleeding. We couldn't tell whether his eye had been punctured. Unfortunately, Dr. Kleinschmidt was home on furlough at the time. At such a time as this, one's heart cries out, "Lord help me now." We are reminded: "God is our refuge and strength, a very present help in trouble" (Ps. 46:1). "...from whence cometh my help. My help cometh from the Lord, which made heaven and earth" (Ps. 121:1-2).

I immediately sent for Jen, who was at the women's school, and we rushed over to the hospital to seek the help of our efficient nurse, Mary White. She did all she possibly could to clean up the wound but could not determine if the eye had been damaged. She suggested we take him to our A.I.M. Kuluva Hospital in Uganda. Ronnie became conscious and was in pain so Mary gave him medications to relieve the pain and to quiet him. We drove 120 miles to Aru and across the Uganda border to the hospital.

Fortunately both Dr. Ted and Dr. Peter Williams were on hand. Peter, who specialized in eyes, determined that the eye had not been punctured, but he could not determine if the cornea was detached. We stayed in the hospital with Ronnie for more than a week. Nursing him was a day-and-night watch because he would try to rub his eye. Both arms had to be immobilized by binding magazines around his elbows, and his pain was suppressed by strong medication.

The whole experience caused us to completely cast ourselves at the feet of the Lord. On occasions I walked some of the secluded paths on the station and got down on my knees, pouring out my heart to the Lord. For a period of time we wondered whether Ronnie would pull through. One night as Jen and I were having our devotions together, our reading was from Psalm 116. It was the "balm of Gilead" to our troubled souls. Every word seemed to be amplified and came through loud and clear.

> *I love the Lord, because He hath heard my voice and my supplications. Because He hath inclined His ear unto me, therefore will I call upon Him as long as I live. The sorrows of death compassed me, and the pains of hell gat hold upon me: I found trouble and sorrow. Then called I upon the name of the Lord; O Lord, I beseech Thee, deliver my*

soul. Gracious is the Lord, and righteous; yea, our God is merciful. The Lord preserveth the simple: I was brought low, and He helped me. Return unto thy rest, O my soul; for the Lord hath dealt bountifully with thee (Psalm 116:1-7).

We were melted in prayer together and the Lord, in His grace, answered. The swelling subsided enough for the doctor to determine that Ronnie did not have a detached retina, but as a result of all he went through he lost a lot of weight. He looked "skinny" in comparison with his normal robust self, and it took him a full year to begin to get back his strength. The wounded eye gave the appearance of drooping, and we thought he would be marred for life; but in the goodness of the Lord, even that returned to normal after a number of years. Going through various experiences similar to this with the children caused us to realize how much we needed to put our trust in the One who is *Jehovah Shammah* (the Lord is there). He was there to meet our need on every occasion.

As each of the children grew up, home-schooling became part of the daily routine. Jen taught them from kindergarten through first grade, using the Calvert course. She did this in addition to her responsibilities in the women's school. The Mission's general policy was to send the children to Rethy Academy when they were seven years of age. Rethy was a beautiful station, located among the rolling highlands at an altitude of about six thousand feet. The climate was excellent and the land fertile for growing all sorts of vegetables and potatoes. Having a hospital and medical personnel there made it an ideal place for the school. Missionary teachers and house-parents taught and ministered to the students, not only in the classroom and dormitories but also in sports and social programs. This school cared for their academic needs through the ninth grade, after which they would complete their high school education at Rift Valley Academy in Kenya. The school term was approximately 13 weeks with 5 weeks of vacation at home with the family. As parents we had much to be grateful for. The greatest problem we and our children were confronted with was the matter of separation. As missionaries, we went through this with our parents when we left our home shores and loved ones to fulfill the Lord's call to us. Now to be separated from our children at such an early age was traumatic. We not only felt the emotional pain for ourselves but also for the children.

Each of them responded differently. To some it was devastating. They felt forsaken and believed that the close bond with the family was being broken. Lois led the way and each of the others followed when their time came. Meeting them at the end of the school term was always a jubilant occasion. Although we had wonderful family times during their five weeks vacation, we knew that it would end too soon. Building up friendships with their classmates eventually alleviated a portion of the heartache, but only to some extent.

We tried to make school vacation a good family time together. As we traveled the two hundred miles back to our station, the children reveled in word games. During our third term the route we followed took us through three countries, Zaire, Uganda, and Sudan. The scenery was beautiful and things happened that demanded our attention. Crossing the great White Nile on the

Pakquach pontoon ferry was always an interesting experience. The ferry was not motorized. Therefore, it had to be poled upstream against the current along the bank of the large body of water. Then as we navigated toward the center of the river, the swift current carried us speedily downstream and the skilled boatmen paddled as fast as they could to reach the opposite shore and safely into its mooring where we disembarked.

Then we would be on our way through about 25 miles of animal reserve, which was a real treat and many times produced some excitement. We drove through nature's zoological gardens, beholding the beauty of God's handiwork in the form of small wiry Thompson's gazelles, the graceful bodies of various species of deer, waterbuck, and the gigantic black buffalo whose massive horns were a threat to any intruder.

The herds of elephant were a sight to behold as they moved slowly over the terrain. Sometimes we encountered them on the road and had them both in front of and behind our car. Blowing the horn and beating on the sides of the car generally cleared the way. Sometimes we met them suddenly just around a curve in the road and we were mutually startled. The huge ears of the elephant would spread out like wings as he charged to protect himself, then hastily putting on the brakes our car skidded over the gravel road to a stop. We, of course, were greatly relieved when he backed off.

It was also interesting to see the beautiful white egrets walking on the backs of the elephants. They were friends of the elephants because they ate the ticks off their backs. Many times a large number of egrets would roost on a small tree. They looked like the decorations on a Christmas tree as they waited for their next meal train to come along!

When the children were with us for their vacation period, all sorts of indoor and outdoor games were part of our schedule. The tennis court next to our home was in continuous use, and on occasions I took the boys hunting. Christmas was always a special time and we tried to prepare for it in advance so that presents would be on hand. Packages came from family and friends in the homeland. Once, during World War II when mails were erratic, no packages arrived, but the missionaries on the station rallied to the cause and provided all sorts of goodies. We searched out gifts from our five-year supply of clothing, shoes, etc. that had been stored away for future use. They were wrapped up in holiday paper and received with great anticipation and an understanding spirit. We always had a Christmas tree. It was not a pine tree because there were none in our area in Sudan, but with ornaments and homemade decorations, it was a good replica of those we had in the homeland. On one occasion we searched for an appropriate green tree, which was hard to find during the dry season. Fortunately, we did locate one that had long slender leaves. We decorated it beautifully just before going to bed. On Christmas morning Mother Nature added something to our tree display that we never expected. All the branches and long slender leaves were vigorously stretching and pointing in the direction of the tropical sun coming through the window. It looked like something that would get first prize in a modern art show!

MK's (Missionary Kids) or Third World Kids, as they are referred to today, may miss out on some of the privileges children have in the homeland. However, they are compensated by many other exotic experiences. They have the thrill of traveling on a small launch up the Nile River toward Murchinson Falls and getting a wonderful view of all sorts of wildlife standing in the bushes at the water's edge, satisfying their thirst. Families of hippo frolic in the water, sometimes with their mouths wide open, while others are sleepily submerged with their nostrils slightly above the water's level. Scores of crocodiles can be seen basking in the sun along the shore or crowded together on small islands in the middle of the river, many of them with their jaws wide open, ready for action. When our boat was steered in the direction of one island, about twenty of them sprang forward and slithered into the water and out of sight. We couldn't get close to the base of the falls because the water was turbulent with whirlpools, however, we were able to walk overland to the top of Murchinson Falls, and what a sight to behold! The whole White Nile converged through a huge 19-foot gap in the rocks. There was a small bridge that spanned the gap where we could stand and see this massive amount of water pass through, watching it hit one side and then the other of the walled rock, and then drop several hundred feet into the large basin below, which was a swirling mass. As a family we stood there and marveled at the wonders of God's creation.

Traveling back and forth to the field was an education in itself that took us through Egypt, the land of the Pharaohs, Sphinx, and pyramids. In Greece we climbed over the ruins of the Acropolis and stood where the apostle Paul had preached on Mars Hill, overlooking the city of Athens; then we traveled through Italy with its rich Italian culture. We were enamored by what we saw in Rome, with its amphitheater and the gruesome stories of Christian martyrs, as well the beauties of its church architecture and the grandeur of Michelangelo's paintings. We sailed on the historic Rhine River in Germany and climbed the Alps in Switzerland. We visited England, the land of my forebears, which glories in its historical past. During the war years we were rerouted via Nigeria and Liberia, then by flying boat on to Brazil, to experience the warmth of another friendly Portuguese culture. This journey was made on 11 different planes and it took us two and one-half months to finally arrive in New York.

S.S. United States. World record Atlantic crossing.

Imagine having the privilege of traveling on the fastest passenger boat in the world, the *S.S. United States*, on its maiden voyage crossing the Atlantic Ocean from the east to the west. This was thrilling to our four kids, and to mom and dad, who had just come out of the heart of the bush country in Africa. We were booked on it by our British travel agent, and even in cabin class! It was a beautiful ship and there was a lot to see and do. The ship had already broken the speed record from the United States to England and was now hoping to do the same on its return journey. Each day we looked at the bulletin board that listed the special events of the day, and it so happened that the next day was Sunday. I said to

Jen, "I wonder what celebrity will be speaking at the church service." I believe this was to be the first public service held on the ship, since the voyage from the west to the east was on weekdays. After making my comment to Jen, the thought came to me, "Suppose you are asked to speak. What kind of a message would you give?" I mentioned this to Jen, but since our British travel agent had booked us under the name Mr. and Mrs. Langford and family, and I was not recorded on the passenger list as a "Reverend." I felt there was little chance of my being asked to speak. In spite of this, I felt constrained to go and prepare a message. While alone in the cabin praying and preparing, the telephone rang and the voice said, "Is this Reverend Langford?" I answered, "Yes," and he continued, "This is the ship's purser. We are thinking of the Sunday church service and wondering if you would take charge." I knew this was from the Lord so I said, "I would be glad to." Then he gave me the general details as to the time and place it would be held.

In making arrangements for the meeting, I felt it would be good to have other clergy participate. Two others agreed to read the Scripture and lead in prayer. The bandmaster of the ship's orchestra asked if I would like to have them play a special number. I said, "By all means," because that meant that they would be on hand for the message.

Prior to the time of the service I had another call from the purser. He said there was a lady aboard who had the creamated remains of her husband and had asked permission to bury them at sea. He said that would mean slowing the ship down for the occasion, and they would like to avoid that because they were trying to set a new speed record. He asked me if I would take care of this and gave me the name and phone number of the lady. I called her and made arrangements to speak with her following the Sunday morning service.

All the passengers of the ship, regardless of what class they were traveling in, were invited to the service. When the hour arrived, the audience packed the large designated area. I was thrilled at the opportunity. The other clergy preferred not to lead the meeting, so I carried the responsibility and was very conscious of the Lord's enabling. All the preliminaries went off well and the orchestra performed excellently. I spoke on the theme,"Lord, Here Am I," focusing on the expression that Moses, Abraham, and Isaiah had used. I had real liberty in the proclamation of the Word, challenging hearts to make the same commitment for salvation, for dedication, and for service. I couldn't help but feel that what had taken place was the Lord's plan and for His glory.

Following the service, the dear lady who was interested in the burial of her husband's remains, introduced herself to me. She told me that she and her husband had met while traveling at sea, and it was his dying wish that he be buried at sea. She wanted this to be a private ceremony, without slowing the ship down. So I arranged to meet her after lunch. We went to the back of the ship where I read several passages of Scripture and led in prayer. Then, she threw the urn of her beloved husband's remains into the sea.

It was a privilege for the family to be on this historic maiden voyage of the S.S. United States. It was an exciting experience. We had been traveling full speed ahead for three days, making our way to New York Harbor. As we crossed the finish line of Ambrose Lighthouse buoy, the band was out on the open deck and played with great exuberance and fanfare. We had broken the world's speed record for crossing the Atlantic from the east to the west.

As we entered the harbor and continued slowly up the Hudson River, we were welcomed by nearly all the ships we passed. They saluted us with the blasts of their whistles. We were escorted by a flotilla of smaller boats that joined the procession and we were greeted by numerous fireboats with their hoses going full blast, sending their spray high into the sky. And helicopters were flying overhead! What a thrill for the family!

As we neared the giant dock, we could see the crowds of people, friends of those on board. The greatest thrill of all was the wonderful welcome of our loved ones and friends who were there to greet us. Now the family was home once again, from the bushland and culture of central Africa to the fast pace of the American culture. America had changed during the five years we were away and presented new challenges to us and our children. However, our confidence was in the Lord who had gone before, knowing that He changeth not and is the same yesterday, today, and forever.

Population explosion
with spouses and ten grandchildren.

Chapter 12

Outreach Via the Home Base

Jen and I were very happy in our work in the Sudan and we thoroughly enjoyed the fellowship of our missionary colleagues. Our four stations made steady progress. This doesn't mean that we were without problems. We had weathered the mutiny and the struggles that led to independence and the establishing of the Muslim government. We had a good rapport with our Sudanese church and its leadership, and as a team we were on the "cutting edge" of outreach to many tribes that were without a witness; the opportunity for expansion was a challenge.

It was at such a time as this that Dr. Ralph Davis, who had served as U.S. Director for about 15 years and was now the elected International General Secretary, wrote to me on behalf of the American Home Council. He asked me if I would prayerfully consider the possibility of being appointed as the U.S. Director of the Mission.

This came as a surprise. It was an honor and privilege even to be considered for the position, but our hearts were thrilled with the tremendous opportunities before us in the Sudan. A change like that would greatly affect our ministry, our lives, and our family. We wanted to be in the place of the Lord's choosing. Therefore, Jen and I earnestly prayed for His guidance according to the instruction given in His Word: "Trust in the Lord with all thine heart; and lean not unto thine own understanding. In all thy ways acknowledge Him and He shall direct thy paths" (Prov. 3:5-6). Following a period of waiting upon the Lord, I felt constrained to write to Ralph Davis, expressing my appreciation to the U.S. Council for their invitation and that I would consider it a call from the Lord if all the Councils of the Mission passed it. Inwardly, I wondered if that was even possible, but to my surprise it was approved.

I was given a warm welcome by our American Home Council and I soon learned that they were godly men who had spiritual depth and business acumen, men of integrity and purpose. Dr. Harry Ironside had been the president, followed by Dr. Howard Ferrin, who served for about ten years. Then Dr. Richard Seume, with whom I had a bond of warm fellowship, followed for approximately 25 years. The 15 members of the Council had a good working knowledge of the A.I.M. and they were used of God to build on the firm foundation that had been established by those who had gone on before.

Following my installation in September 1956, I needed to be integrated into the routine of my responsibilities. It was a privilege to have Dr. Ralph Davis as my mentor. Though he was small of stature, he was a giant as a missionary statesman and an innovator

Pearl River office A.I.M.

among his peers in mission circles. He was chosen to be the President of the Interdenominational Foreign Missions Association (IFMA) on nine occasions. He was an excellent communicator and had a warm personality with Irish wit. I thank God for the intimate fellowship I had with him and for the instruction and advice he gave me during the early years of my introduction to the ministry in the Home Office. My assistant and Candidate Secretary at the time was Rev. Joseph Henry, a former pastor who had served as secretary on the A.I.M. Philadelphia committee for a number of years. Our office staff consisted of about 20 who served as secretaries and bookkeepers. Miss Ruth Johnson was the office manager and did an excellent job. At a later date, Rev. August Holm, Dr. John Gration, and Rev Edward Schuit became part of the executive staff, each of whom contributed greatly to our home base operation.

This phase of mission thrust is a vital part of the Lord's work that receives very little publicity or praise.

A.I.M. staff.

It ministers in what people might consider to be mundane, because it relates to administration and management. But it is very important to both the home base and the field operations. It deals with personnel, staff, missionaries, candidates, home constituency, pastors, churches, public relations, and finances, and works with other organizations, etc. These specific categories are departmentalized and come under the jurisdiction of the Sending Home Council, which is ultimately responsible to the International Council. However, policies of the mission are not dictated by the I.C.; they are determined by prayerful consultation with all the field and sending Councils representatives in collaboration with our family of missionaries. Mentioning these few facts gives a mini overview of a maxi operation.

Each morning the staff gathered in the office for prayer. This was basic preparation for the tasks to be performed and for our relationships with each other. The various phases of the work and special needs were remembered. This made us a vital part of our missionaries' lives and of the national church.

International Council.

Serving in the home office enlarged my vision from the challenge and burden of only one field to all our fields and enabled me to feel the pulse and heartbeat of the mission. Visiting our Sending Councils in Canada, England, Australia, and South Africa and making contact with missionaries and national leaders on the field accomplished this.

It was stimulating to visit our "troops" out on the front lines of advance in enemy territory. Although there are many similarities between our fields, there are also distinct differences. This is also true of the structure and policies of the various governments with whom we must deal. Governments that are Muslim or communist in background are restrictive. Some declare themselves socialistic but not Marxist. Others claim to be a democracy with voting choices made within a one-party legislative body. They are generally cooperative and appreciate mission programs. Today, independent countries are pressured to be more democratic by having plurality of political parties. No matter what the personal opinions of missionaries may be, they must divorce themselves from the politics of the land and give

Inter-field Council.

Outreach to home constituency via banquets.

themselves to the task of planting and building the Church of Jesus Christ.

During the early formative years of the Church, the mission exercised complete control. The people were primitive and had little or no schooling. The pioneers in each area actually began to lay the foundations of the work from "scratch", and they sought to fulfill measurable goals. It was thrilling to see the Lord work as the Church grew and expanded. Primary schools prepared the way for the upper grades, and eventually high school and teacher training colleges were established. Literally thousands of the students came to Christ through our general education program, which included the teaching of Scripture. Bible colleges and seminaries prepared local leadership for the Church. The years of active experience of these leaders in the ministry equipped them to fulfill our ultimate goal, that of granting complete autonomy to the national churches. The process for reaching that status was different in each country. In some areas it was achieved in a smooth transition; in others it took lengthy discussion and negotiations with church leaders and our missionary body. It was bathed in prayer and eventually an autonomous church was born in each of our major fields. It was a thrill to be involved in these negotiations and to see God work out so many intricate and sometimes difficult details for His glory.

Africa is a vast continent divided into 47 countries. God has used missionaries to plant the Church in each one. Because the Church of Christ crosses all national and tribal boundaries, pastors and missionaries alike felt that an evangelical fellowship should be established. This fellowship would link the leadership of the various countries together for mutual encouragement and spiritual benefit to each other.

It started in a small way in Kenya and gradually spread to surrounding countries. Rev. Kenneth Downing, who had been involved as the Interfield Secretary of the Africa Inland Mission and previously had intimate contact with all the Africa Inland Church leadership in our various fields, was asked to become the first General Secretary of the organization, The Association of Evangelicals for Africa and Madagascar (AEAM). It was a privilege to be on an ad hoc committee, with Ken and Dr. Clyde Taylor, to draw up the beginnings of the first constitution. As Ken met with the church leaders in various areas of Africa, he created interest in this new development.

Acceptance of a new continent-wide organization was slow at first. National leaders wanted to be sure that their local autonomy would not be affected, but after seeing a practical outworking and the benefits of a unified plan of operation, a gradual reception of it grew in country after country. This effectively strengthened the bond and thrust of the evangelical movement throughout all Africa.

With the groundwork laid, Ken handed the baton of leadership over to Dr. Byang Kato, who was a tower of spiritual strength for its continual growth and development until his untimely death. Presently, Dr. Tokunboh Adeyemo has continued to follow hard in his footsteps, providing excellent leadership as the executive officer, together with Dr. Samuel Odanaike, a keen businessman from West Africa, who was Chairman of the Council. Great strides are being made. The periodic general and regional conferences that are held with representatives from all over the continent are evidence of this. With warmhearted collaboration, the Church of Christ continues to move forward at the command of the Lord of the Harvest, who said, "I will build My church" (Mt. 16:18).

Personal contacts with each of our fields kept me up-to-date with the development and trends of the work and afforded opportunity for fellowship with the missionaries and national leaders, who shared their burdens and joys. Dealing with knotty problems was generally balanced by the thrill of giving out the Word, encouraging our colleagues, and ministering to students and national churches. In 1972 the Sudan was just emerging from eight years of civil strife. Thousands had lost their lives and many church leaders and Christians had taken refuge in Uganda or Kenya. A peace agreement was finally signed between General Nimeri of the north and General Lagu of the south. This agreement granted the southerners a measure of autonomy and a southern legislative body that was recognized by the northern government. This signaled the beginning of the return of the refugees and the leaders of the A.I.C.

Visiting the fields to encourage and to be updated.

At this time I obtained permission to get into the Sudan. In Juba I was able to get a ride on a military truck going to Torit. I was exhilarated about actually being back in the Sudan. Upon arrival, I carried my luggage through the town, making my way toward "our home," the house that I had constructed in the 1950's. Many memories flashed through my mind. I remembered how God had enabled us to get established and the good times we had experienced there as a family.

Pastor Nikolau was residing in the home, and he gave me a warm welcome. His brother, Pastor Abednego, was away visiting some of the churches that had been reopened. Pastor Abednego was informed of my arrival and he returned that evening with about five other pastors. After a hearty meal together, we had a wonderful time of fellowship. We rejoiced over the fact that God had answered prayer and brought back a good number of the exiled A.I.C. Sudan Church. We sat up until past midnight, discussing strategy for reestablishing the work in all areas.

I found that they had thought things through thoroughly. Their plans included starting a Bible School to train pastors and opening elementary schools and a clinic. They also looked hopefully for the re-entrance of our missionaries. Together, we sought the Lord's guidance, help, and provision to initiate these plans.

Eventually, a few of the missionaries who had been expelled in 1964 were permitted to return. They were faced with the rugged task of rehabilitation. Buildings had been destroyed, which meant roughing it until reconstruction was completed. Our team was dedicated to the Lord and the difficult task of planting the Church in the arid soil of Sudan began. In the years immediately following this, I was privileged to see the fulfillment of these goals.

Field visits provided the joyous occasion for Jen and me to visit the place of our first love, Aba station and district. AIM/AIR flew us over the familiar territory where we had traveled by foot and bicycle in years gone by. We were even able to land on the station and were greeted warmly by nationals and missionaries with whom we had worked. Their handshakes and enthusiasm were exhilarating. This was home, where Jen and I had met, served, and raised our family.

The church and all its ministries was in the hands of competent national leaders. Bill and Ruth Stough were our host and hostess. When the local population learned of our arrival, a steady stream came to give us greetings. Even Danyele, the elderly leprosy patient, came on crutches with his gift of a chicken. I felt guilty about taking it, but to refuse would have been a breach of etiquette. We spent hours chatting with all who came. Then the elders and leaders on the station gave a formal welcome banquet. It was an hilarious occasion. As we ate, we recalled humorous incidents of our past relations with them. Speaking to a crowded church on the Lord's Day was exciting. Their congregational singing and numerous choir selections were harmonious and sung with gusto. Even the bricks in the church building, constructed in 1940, told a story of God's faithfulness.

The church elders invited me to hold an evangelistic campaign throughout the districts in the bush areas where we had trekked on many occasions in the past. It was an honor! The leaders outlined a plan to visit two locations every day and they sent word ahead to prepare the villages for our arrival. We traveled by pickup truck, accompanied by several pastors and trumpeters. Riding through the bush was slow, as in some places the grass was high. Long before we got to Ataki's village, our first destination, the people were on the path to greet us, and a large crowd of several hundred in the village crowded around to shake hands. It was a gala welcome!

The chapel, a spacious mud brick building, was soon packed to overflowing. The service was well planned. Time was not a concern! Music played a big part in all our meetings. The trumpeters played jubilantly and the people loved to sing. Men sat on one side of the chapel and the women on the other.

It was so good that Jen was with me because the women appreciated her presence. They asked Jen to give a testimony and she spoke with enthusiasm. She asked how many of the women had been in the girls' zeriba (home) when she was there, and it was surprising to see the number of hands raised. Now they were mothers and grandmothers, bearing a testimony in the village. When Jen finished her greetings, a procession of women marched slowly down the aisle to the tune of a hymn and they presented her with a gift, covered with a cloth. As Jen received it, she wondered what it might be, as it was quite heavy. It was a hand-woven basket, filled with rice and about a dozen eggs on top. The whole procedure took place very ceremoniously. Then it was my privilege to give an evangelistic challenge. The response to the invitation given by the African pastor was a cause for praise to the Lord.

While we were in this village, I made inquiry concerning the former village chief, Ataki. I had spoken to him on many occasions in years gone by. He always listened respectfully but never made a decision for Christ. One day he became seriously ill and from all outward appearances he died—at least there were no signs of life—and they prepared him for burial. The grave was dug and his body was brought to the site. Just before the interment, someone noticed a slight movement of his body, and the miraculous outcome was that he was restored to life.

Sometime after this had taken place, I was on a safari that took me through his village. I met him on the path and talked to him about the Lord, reminding him that God had been merciful in sparing his life from eternal judgment. I reminded him that the Lord was giving him another opportunity to receive the Savior, and thus I urged him to do so before it was too late. He listened very intently but did not make a decision at that time. I was so happy to learn, on the occasion of our visit, that he had accepted Christ and bore a good testimony up to the time of his eventual death.

It was also at Ataki's village we were brought into contact with a close friend, Rebeka Kudrodeko. She was brought to the girls' home at Aba as a little orphan girl and she grew up under the tutelage of the older girls. She had come from a village where there was no Christian testimony. During her younger years she was a rascal, always trying to get away with doing as little as possible. The farming chores were supposed to be done by all the girls to provide their own food, and often she had to be disciplined for her failure to complete her share. Today Rebeka is a grown married woman with four children. She also has an orphan child, whom she has nursed from birth. As a Christian, she broke the tradition of the tribe to do this. She said that when she was orphaned, someone cared for her. Now she wanted to do this for this motherless baby. We had such a good visit with her, laughing over her capers of the past and rejoicing when she said jokingly, "The discipline administered years ago really paid off!" Today Rebeka is a radiant servant of the Lord, giving a strong witness in the village of Ataki among the Logo tribe.

That same day we continued our safari to the village of Paramount Chief Ali. This was the first village that I had stayed at as a young new missionary back in 1936. Chief Ali was a warm friend of the missionaries, but the prestige of his position involved drinking native beer and he became an alcoholic. Years later, he received Christ and made Him the Lord of his life. He stopped drinking and the testimony of his stand became well known. Jen and I were looking forward to seeing Ali.

However, on the way we came upon a large wooden bridge that didn't look too safe. We all got out of the truck to make it as light as possible for our driver to negotiate the questionable structure. Unfortunately, one front wheel broke through the bridge. I could see that it would take some time to jack up the front of the car in order to insert a stronger footing. Our national driver had been well trained by Bill Stough, and his experience dictated just what had to be done. I was concerned about the meeting at Chief Ali's. Would we be able to have it as planned? A slight drizzle also dampened our spirits and we sought shelter under one of the trees. One of the trumpeters gave Jen his raincoat. All the men applied themselves to the task of cutting large poles to repair the bridge.

As time passed, I came to the conclusion that I should borrow a bicycle and push on toward Ali's village, which was about eight miles away. This would be like old times, for I had biked over that path on many occasions; but it had been about 35 years before! I started off with enthusiasm, but I soon found out that the bike was old and had bent pedals, which made pushing rather awkward. After traveling about four miles over a rough and rugged hilly path, I could feel my age creeping up on me. When I came to one village, I decided to stop for a rest. I must have looked faint because one of the village women offered me some oranges. The oranges resuscitated me so that I could continue on, and in due time I arrived at my destination.

Chief Ali and all the people were thrilled at my arrival and they gave me a warm welcome. I felt like I had just finished a marathon, but the thrill of being there helped to revive me. The African pastor decided I needed some food, which was gladly accepted.

After about an hour I felt we should start the meeting because we didn't know when the truck would arrive. The chapel was soon filled and the chief had a special seat of honor. Shortly after the service started, the truck and all its occupants arrived and received a jubilant welcome. It was good to see Jen, safe and sound. With the Lord's help, she took all the happenings in her stride. We resumed the meeting again with the welcome addition of our five trumpeters, who gave real zest to our worship.

Lo and behold, in the midst of our song service, one of the village women joined the brass ensemble with a unique instrument. It was a long crooked car tail pipe, and with real enthusiasm she added an "umppa-umppa" sound to the orchestral notes. In Africa it just didn't seem to be too out-of-place. No doubt, it could be added to the list of all the Old Testament instruments used to praise the Lord!

Giving the Word to this crowd was a thrill, and again God worked within hearts and decisions were made. Following the meeting, the team all sat down to a sumptuous feast and fellowship. We arrived back at Aba station that night, weary of body, but grateful for the privilege of being in the service of the King.

This was the pattern of the meetings each day. Our travels took us into all the areas surrounding Aba. We sought to be an encouragement to the pastors who were faithfully holding forth the Word of Life. Multitudes were reached and about two hundred made decisions for Christ.

The Lord used each of our many visits to our fields to make a spiritual impact upon those to whom we ministered. He also used these visits to impact our own lives, and the thrill of it continues to live on.

Chapter 13

It Is a Battle

Peter Cameron Scott, the founder of the African Inland Mission, ended his first encounter with pioneer missionary service in lower Congo when he was stricken with malaria and blackwater fever. He was carried out of the country on a stretcher and brought back to England by boat. He marvelously survived the trip, and on the evening he arrived, he was welcomed by a group of enthusiastic missionary candidates who were being entertained by friends in London. Peter was so weak that he had to be helped out of the cab. He was supported by a strong arm as he entered the room and sat down among the outgoing recruits. In his weakened condition, he said, "Well friends, you are going forth; I have come back. It is no child's play; it is a battle!"

What happened in the years that followed proved the reality of his prophetic statement. During the period of Scott's recuperation in the United States, he learned of the multitudes in East Africa who had never heard the gospel. The more he researched this, the

First party of missionaries
Peter Cameron Scott seated second from left.

greater his burden became. He appealed to his Mission
Board to open a new work, but they lacked funds. Undaunted, he felt constrained to proceed by faith. He
gathered a group of godly men, who made up the Board
of Directors, and they founded the Africa Inland Mission in 1895. He launched forth with a party of eight
missionaries who made their way to Mombasa in Kenya. When preparations were completed they pressed
northward into the interior, seeking to fulfill Peter's
goal of planting stations from Mombasa to Lake Chad.
Their three hundred-mile trek took them through
treacherous tribal areas and they planted their first
mission station at Nzawi, among the Wakamba tribe. In
the first 15 months, 4 stations were started. This was
no small task. Malaria and blackwater fever plagued

that first party, necessitating the return of some to the homeland. Peter himself came down with repeated attacks of malaria and succumbed to the disease after only a year and a half on the field. Actually, the mission was whittled down to one lone missionary and it seemed as though the mission was about to fold up.

The Council in America met together in an emergency session to give consideration to the future of the work. Some felt that the death of the founder and the departure of the other missionaries was the finger of God calling the work to a halt. It was at that time that Dr. A.T. Pierson, that great man of God and a member of the Council, turned to all the men present and said, "Gentlemen, the hallmark of God on any life or work is death. God has given us the hallmark; now is the time to go forward." This was God's challenge to that early Council and God had His Joshua in the Council. The president, Charles Hurlburt, felt constrained to accept the challenge. He took up the torch that Peter Cameron Scott was called upon to lay down. This resulted in a tremendous new outreach and eventually the fulfillment of Scott's vision.

We are aware of the fact that, throughout the history of mankind, there have been wars and rumors of wars. In each conflict the opposing sides endeavor, by every means possible, to ascertain the strength of their enemies and plan their strategy accordingly. Our Lord referred to this when He said, "Or suppose a king is about to go to war against another king. Will he not first sit down and consider whether he is able with ten thousand men to oppose the one coming against him with twenty thousand?" (Lk. 14:31 NIV)

As Christians, it is wise for us to do the same thing as we face our archenemy, satan. Thank God, the Captain of our salvation knows all about him, his wiles, cunning, and subtleties; therefore it is most necessary that we get our instructions and guidelines from Him.

The Scriptures give a detailed description of the enemy. He is spoken of as "the prince of the power of the air" (Eph. 2:2), "the god of this age" (2 Cor. 4:4 NIV), "the prince of this world" (Jn. 12:31), and a "roaring lion" (1 Pet. 5:8). He has great organizational ability and his purpose is to thwart the plan of God. He endeavored to do that when he tested the Son of God in the wilderness (see Lk. 4:1-13), but was defeated with the "Sword of the Spirit" (Eph. 6:17)

The Word of God reveals that he is a deceiver (Rev. 20:10), blinds men to the truth (2 Cor. 4:4), instigates false doctrine (1 Tim. 4:1-3), hinders the work of God (1 Thess. 2:18), resists the prayers of God's servants (Dan. 10:12-13), undermines the sanctity of the home (1 Cor. 7:3-5), causes division in the Church of Christ (Rom. 16:17-20), and he is a tempter (Mt. 4:1). Both missionaries and national Christians would readily agree we have a formidable foe. *It is a battle.*

We are grateful for the fact that the Bible reveals much about our spiritual warfare. In the very beginning we see that old serpent, the devil, rearing his head in the garden of Eden (Gen. 3:1-7). Down through the course of history he has continued to seek those he might devour. Many of the prophets in the Old Testament suffered at the hand of the enemy as they sought to carry out the will of God.

Onslaughts from the adversary may take on various forms. Jacob said of his son Joseph, who had been persecuted by his brethren, "...With bitterness archers attacked him; they shot at him with hostility" (Gen. 49:23 NIV). But the hand of the Almighty blessed him (Gen. 49:23-26).

Nehemiah was burdened concerning the sins of Israel, which had resulted in the destruction of Jerusalem, and he was called of God to rebuild the wall of the city (see Neh. 1–2). In doing so, he faced all sorts of opposition from the enemies of the Lord, who sought to use every diabolical method to hinder the task that was assigned to him. African church leaders and missionaries face a similar problem as they pursue the work of building the Church of Christ. But God, in answer to fervent prayer, prevailed on behalf of Nehemiah, causing the wrath of man to praise Him (see Ps. 76:10) and "...the wall was finished...in fifty and two days" (Neh. 6:15). In spite of the confrontations on the mission field, one day the victorious task of the Church of Christ will also be completed.

The Lord told His disciples, "And ye shall be hated of all men for My name's sake" (Lk. 21:17). The Book of Acts verifies that they were persecuted and scattered abroad. The apostle Paul testifies concerning this when he was attacked in numerous ways on his three missionary journeys. He also spoke of his "thorn in the flesh" as being buffeted by satan (2 Cor. 12:7). Therefore, he forewarned all Christians: "For we wrestle not against flesh and blood, but against principalities, against powers, against the rulers of the darkness of this world, against spiritual wickedness in high places" (Eph. 6:12); and his solution was to—"Put on the whole armour of God, that ye may be able to stand against the wiles of the devil" (Eph. 6:11).

When we encroach upon the enemy's stronghold, he will contest every inch of territory we endeavor to take in the name of the Lord. Often his first attack will be on our bodies. I experienced this personally, arriving in Africa with pneumonia, and within a month coming down with amoebic dysentery and then numerous attacks of malaria. Many times this is the pattern followed by the enemy shortly after the arrival of a new missionary on the field, causing physical weakness and discouragement.

Some conflicts faced by missionaries are problems they have with themselves and the personality differences they may experience with their colleagues. Two people who come from different backgrounds and life styles may be assigned to work together, having no choice of other companionship. Leaders may clash over differing ideas concerning policy and procedures, causing strained relations. Solutions do not always come easily, especially when godly servants of the Lord like Paul and Barnabas are involved. Such difficulties must be bathed in prayer, seeking answers from the Lord.

One evening during a Congo Field Conference gathering, John Stauffacher, one of our pioneer missionaries, realized some of the personality problems we younger missionaries would face. He spoke informally to us "young bucks," and told us of an experience he had many years before when he and Charles Hurlburt, the General Director, were on safari together. Both of these men were stalwart godly leaders that had been greatly used of the Lord. He told us that something came up, causing a division between them that was so strong they didn't even speak to each other. It became so serious that John considered separating himself from Mr. Hurlburt and the A.I.M. Then one night, after they had gone to bed, John awakened and saw Charles Hurlburt kneeling beside his cot, pouring out his heart to the Lord in silent prayer. Mr. Hurlburt was not aware that John had awakened. The Lord used this to speak to John's heart and the breach was healed. From the next morning on they never mentioned their problem again and they worked harmoniously together being mightily used in their exploits for God. As John told this, it made a deep impression on me, helping me to realize that the answer to my own problems and struggles was to be found at the feet of the Master, giving heed to the exhortation, "Take heed unto thyself..." (1 Tim. 4:16a).

Traditionally, the people of Africa live in constant fear of an attack from evil spirits, and they will go to whatever extent is necessary to appease them. They may seek the help of the village witch doctor because they believe he is in contact with the spirits and wields the power to bless or curse, to heal or to kill. It was said that the fear of demonic powers, manifested by a woman witch doctor, hindered the growth of the church at Nzawi, the first station of the A.I.M. in Kenya, for many years.

African Christians face all sorts of opposition from their tribe because they have renounced the religious animist traditions of their forefathers. It is an enlightening experience to discuss these problems with African pastors and evangelists. Sometimes, with reticence, they will tell of being attacked by spirit beings in their houses at night. For instance, an outstanding Christian woman leader, married to a pastor, sought the help of a missionary. She told the missionary that this was happening so continually in their home that they couldn't get enough sleep. Even the children screamed, claiming someone was after them. The family was exhausted. It was suggested that a group of Christians should meet in their home during the night for a special prayer meeting, seeking the Lord's intervention. They did this unitedly and earnestly pouring out their hearts to the Lord, claiming the protecting and victorious power of the blood of Jesus. The Lord answered by eliminating the attack and granting complete deliverance and peace, confirming the fact that "God is our refuge and strength, a very present help in trouble" (Ps. 46:1).

There are times when the enemy's strategy is to attack from within the church itself. The apostle Paul struggled with this in some of the churches he had planted and satan continues to use the same tactics. On

Animistic spirit house where gifts of food are placed.

one occasion the entire Aru Church in Zaire arose in rebellion. It began as the result of a new government regulation requiring the signature of the missionary in the tax books of each individual to show evidence of their residence at the mission. Some of the nationals, at the grass roots level, concluded that the missionary was responsible for this and became irate. Thus, a small spark ignited into a great conflagration and spread like wildfire over the entire station. The events that took place were unbelievable. Some of the excellent church leaders were evidently coerced by peer pressure into the rebellion. They wouldn't listen to reason, as neither the mission nor missionaries had anything to do with the regulation. The people on the station were stirred into a riotous frenzy and the missionaries were threatened with machetes swished angrily before their faces. The instigators wouldn't even allow girls to carry water to their homes. Actually Christians from another station, on hearing of this, volunteered to carry water as an expression of their concern and love. The intimidation was such that no one dared to attend church services, and the leaders would not meet with the missionaries to pray or to discuss the problem.

I had just come over from the Sudan and happened to stop at Aru for a visit, when I learned what was taking place. It eventually became evident that prayer and prayer alone was the answer. The missionaries on the station decided to meet daily to pray throughout the day. It was a time of wrestling against the principalities and powers of darkness. Finally, after days of waiting upon the Lord, the first sign of a breakthrough came when one of the leading pastors came to the prayer session and told how God had been dealing with him through the reading of the Scriptures. He showed deep contrition, confessed his sin, and then joined in the prayer meetings. Taking this step endangered his life, because threats were made by the dissidents. Later, a second pastor returned, and gradually others joined in the same fashion.

A church conference had been planned and the date had been set before the blow-up. Roy Brill, who was in charge of the station, asked me if I would speak at that conference, but he wondered whether anyone would come. However, it was decided to proceed with the plans. I remember an experience I had the night after I had been invited to minister at the conference. I was staying in the station guest house alone. During the course of the night I awakened and became aware of, what seemed to be, an evil presence in the room (which is difficult to explain). I didn't feel afraid, but I decided to get up. I lit a small kerosene lantern and began reading the Scriptures and having a time of prayer. As I continued, the evil presence left and I had real peace. Then I asked the Lord to guide me as to what He would have me to speak on at the conference, which was to take place several weeks from then. That same night the Lord gave me the outline for each of the seven messages that would be given, and the theme "…choose you this day whom ye will serve…" (Josh. 24:15).

I had to return to the Sudan and then come back to Aru for the conference. The first gathering took place on a Sunday. We went to the meeting with much prayer, not knowing if anyone would show up. God answered our prayers and the large church was nearly packed with those who had been in rebellion. We learned that they came out of curiosity to see and hear what was going to take place. I had real liberty as I gave each of the messages and I did not mention the divisive problem. My thrust was a "Thus saith the Lord!" Outwardly, nothing exceptional happened and everyone was attentive. However, the response came following the conference. Many others joined the prayer group and confessed how they had sinned against the Lord. Gradually, over a period of time, the breach was healed. It was a humbling experience for the missionaries and the entire church. Eventually it proved to be a blessing, and resulted in the church bearing a stronger testimony. It was a victory that can only be attributed to God's answering fervent prayer.

In the work of the Lord, confrontation with opposing factors is to be expected. Sometimes these come as a result of conflict with certain tribal customs. Much in their culture is very commendable, but there are areas that are in definite contradiction to the teaching of Scripture. On occasion, the church in Africa has experienced clashes and sometime warlike attacks because of the stand the church takes on Christian truth that is in opposition to certain tribal traditions.

The Mau Mau uprising exploded into a great conflict that took the lives of many Christians. It was a result of the stand that the church took against female circumcision and the serious ill effects that this practice had on women. The elders of the Kukuyu tribe felt that this was an invasion of their ancient rites and they fought violently to preserve it. It was a demonic conflict.

The government brought in strong forces to suppress it and thousands were interned in Mau Mau prison camps. The church responded with the Word of God. The Pocket Testament League was used in a wonderful way at that time. They worked in conjunction with the Africa Inland Church to proclaim the gospel in prison camps and distributed the Gospel of John in national languages to massive crowds in Kenya and throughout all central and east Africa. Their ministry resulted in thousands coming to the Lord.

Many times when pagan men or women become Christians their new way of life provokes the wrath of the tribe, and they are harassed by close relatives who fear the vengeance of the spirit world. Pastor Gidona, one of our fine young leaders at Aba, said his relatives brought pressure to bear upon him because his wife had not given birth to any boys. They said it was because he had not followed the tribal custom of having his four front lower teeth removed. He told them he wouldn't acquiesce to their taunts. When his next child was born, it was a boy. Gidona said that when this happened, he got on his bicycle and rode 50 miles out to his village to announce that a boy had been born. Then he pointed to his four lower teeth that were still intact! He repeated this when the next baby boy arrived. Testimonies such as these strengthens the gospel witness.

The indulgence in native beer, which flows freely in the villages, towns, and cities, results in village brawls that sometimes end in serious injuries or the loss of life. Knowing the havoc it causes, the Africa Inland Church has sought to uphold a scriptural standard of prohibition for those who become part of the family of God. There have been times when this was challenged in the native court.

When a married woman receives Christ as her Savior and grows in the Lord, she may face a confrontation with an unbelieving husband because her standards are now different from his. One Christian wife, who felt that she should obey the Lord rather than man, refused to make beer for her husband and, therefore, was beaten by him. He reasoned that his wife was his property; he had purchased her by paying the dowry that was requested by her parents. The wife felt that making beer compromised her testimony and, therefore, she continued to refuse. The husband felt he had a good case against his wife and, therefore, appealed to the paramount chief, who judged the woman guilty and placed a fine upon her. She joyfully paid the fine, but she continued to renege on making beer. Rather than give in on such a crucial case, the chief decided to bring this to the attention of a government official. When he came on the scene, he ordered her to make beer, but she refused. She felt it was more honorable to be obedient to the Lord. The official decided that, as his judgment upon her, he would give her a heavy task to perform. He told her to cut down a large tree with a machete, which was no small task. Without a question, she started to hack away, to the tune of a hymn, "Glory to His name." She went through verse after verse in the Bangala language, swinging her machete to the rhythm of the hymn. Every phrase testified to the power of the gospel...

> Down at the cross where my Saviour died,
> Down where for cleansing from sin I cried,
> There to my heart was the blood applied,
> Glory to His name.

And then she followed with the chorus,

> Glory to His name, glory to His name,
> There to my heart was the blood applied,
> Glory to His name.

This humble woman was a living testimony of the reality of the message. She repeated the hymn, verse after verse, over and over again as she worked away. Finally, the large tree toppled over. When she told the official that she still would not brew beer, he, peeved at her attitude, ordered her to cut down a second tree. She went through the same procedure, undaunted by the severity of the task, and the tree finally fell to the ground. The official was amazed and frustrated to the extent that he got in his car and left!

The final outcome of this was that her faithful witness won her husband to the Lord. Thus, the lives and vibrant thrust of Christian women continues to grow, and they are literally tools in the Master's hand, bringing "Glory to His name." There are over forty thousand of them in Zaire and Central African Republic, united under the banner of "Women of Good News."

Each time we traveled to the Central African Republic, whether by car and then dugout canoe across the Mbomou River, or by flying directly to Obo, nearly five hundred miles from Bunia in Zaire, we always felt that we had arrived at "the end of the line" in the very heart of Africa. Our pioneer missionaries trekked that distance on foot or bicycle; then some graduated to a motorcycle with a sidecar. C.A.R. was a remote, rugged area and churches were planted around four stations, scattered over several hundred miles. God had blessed the efforts of the missionaries, and the church was born out of paganism, which is still prevalent in the villages. Occasionally cults spring up, gain popularity for a while, and strongly oppose Christianity.

I participated in sessions with the elders of the church in C.A.R. on many occasions, and there were always knotty problems to be considered. The church struggled with such questions as what to do about "underwater witches." When anyone drowned in the Mbomou River, the Zande tribe in that area did not

Women of Good News.

attribute it to an accident, but to *akpiri* or water witches who, according to tradition, lead their victims to the water, pull them in, and kill them. If a canoe overturned and a number lost their lives, this created a panic among the people because a sorcerer was asked to determine who was guilty of the crime. Those that were accused were beaten until they confessed and many died in the process or starved to death in prison. Missionaries have long protested belief in the *akpiri* and the violent action taken against those suspected of being involved in magical murder. They have been told that, as foreigners, they have no right to interfere.

Church leaders who have dared to speak out against this are publicly scorned and ridiculed because some government officials give credibility to the fears of the people and publicly endorse the tradition. Therefore, many local pastors have resorted to silence. This is an example of the spiritual problems that the church is confronted with.

The power of the Word of God and fervent prayer break the stronghold the tribal traditions have on the people and encourage pastors and Christians to take a strong stand by applying the authority of the Scriptures as a bulwark against the deceptive powers of the enemy.

Peter Cameron Scott spoke out of experience when he said to the enthusiastic missionary candidates, "It is a battle." However, the Lord reminds us "the battle is not yours but God's" (2 Chron. 20:15c). The struggle missionaries and national pastors face against the forces of darkness calls for faithful prayer warriors to join the conflict and lay hold upon God in the same manner that Moses, Aaron, and Hur did on behalf of

Joshua and the army of Israel in their war with the Amalekites. The battle strategy against the enemies of the Lord was a cooperative team effort between those on the mountaintop and those in the midst of the turbulent confrontation even "until the going down of the sun" and the Lord wrought a great victory (see Ex. 17:8-15).

Chapter 14

Claim Stakers

Prospecting for gold was a way of life for many of the settlers of the New World. They always were hoping to strike it rich and some did. The discovery of the precious metal in California sparked the "gold rush" of 1849. Families headed westward, risking their lives over treacherous trails and encountering hostile tribes of Indians. They were known as the "forty-niners." Wherever they went, small mining towns sprang up, and when gold was found they would stake their claims, register them with the government office, and then dig and pan for gold. These prospectors were known as "claim stakers." For the most part, they were worldly men who sought to lay up for themselves treasures upon earth.

God is looking for another kind of claim staker. The Scriptures reveal how God guided Moses to choose twelve men from the tribes of Israel to spy out the land of Caanan (Num. 13). Ten of them came back with an evil report that struck fear and unbelief in the hearts of the children of Israel and hindered them from entering in to possess the land God had promised to give them. Two of the spies, Joshua and Caleb, who wholly followed the Lord, urged the people to go in and possess the land. But the word of the ten prevailed, and they wandered about in the wilderness under the judgment of God for another 40 years, and that generation died in the wilderness. Then God raised up their children (whom they thought would be lost in the conflict) and filled their hearts with faith. Under Joshua's leadership they entered the land that overflowed with milk and honey.

When the land was in the process of being divided, Caleb reminded Joshua that Moses had promised him all the land upon which his feet had trodden as an inheritance. Therefore, he said to Joshua, "Now therefore give me this mountain..." (Josh 14:12). Caleb was one of God's "claim stakers." He claimed Mount Hebron by faith in spite of the tremendous obstacles: he was 85 years old and giants were in the land. He defeated the giants, and it became his possession because he wholly followed the Lord. God is still looking for men and women who will wholly follow Him and accept His challenge to become "claim stakers" for God.

The missionary is a spiritual prospector, not looking for gold that perishes, but for the souls of men who are lost, that they might be found and redeemed with the precious blood of Christ. The missionary has heard the call of his Master. As a prospector he has lifted up his eyes and looked on the fields that are white already to harvest (see Jn. 4:35), that he might stake claims for God among the unreached out in the highways and byways of the urban centers of the world, in remote rugged and desert areas, and among those that are hostile to the message of the gospel.

For more than 50 years the northern frontier district of Kenya was declared a closed district by the government. The tribes were said to be too hostile. However, a closed door is always a challenge. It was that to Tom Collins, one of our missionaries, who was handicapped by a heart condition that was evidenced by the blueness of his lips and legs. Nevertheless, in spite of physical obstacles, he sought to penetrate the Pokot and Turkana tribes who were completely unreached. Although he was not permitted to enter the restricted areas, he trekked in the midst of intense heat with a knapsack on his back and sandaled feet. He walked along the borders of these forbidden tribes, hoping to contact any who ventured across the fringes. He touched many individuals, making friendly contacts and giving them the gospel. By faith, he planted the seed, casting his "bread upon the waters" that after many days he might find it again (see Eccles. 11:1). And he did find it!

In 1959 the British government removed the "closed door" restrictions and negotiations were initiated with the tribal leaders to try to gain their favor and entrance among the Turkana, a tribe of 250,000. I was visiting the field at the time, in the capacity of U.S. Director, and I had the opportunity of joining Dr. Dick Anderson and Tom Collins on a safari into this "unreached people" group.

We traveled in a four-wheel-drive Landrover pickup, over what hardly could be called a road, following an unworn track. In many areas we just plowed our way through the bush and over dried-up riverbeds. The road was so rugged that it broke all the engine mounts, and we spent half a day tying the engine in place. We were plagued with tires punctured by the long needles of the thorn bushes and we had so many flats that we actually completed our trip with only one tire patch left! It took us two days to travel 75 miles to Lokori, the "Place of the Camel," which was only a rocky ridge on the bank of a dried-up river. It was a desert wilderness, with not a person or camel in sight. We set up our camp cots on the rocks and spent the night there.

Early the next morning several Turkana warriors appeared on the scene. Both Dick and Tom were able to carry on a conversation with them in Kiswahili. Then some elders of the tribe arrived, and serious discussion took place. We let them know that we would like to come and dwell among them to establish a station where we would build a hospital and school for the purpose of meeting their physical, educational, and spiritual needs. The lengthy dialogue that took place did not have to be punctuated by "time." This was Africa, and time was not a factor. All the details had to be evaluated by the elders, and the decision was finally made that they would be happy to have the Africa Inland Church and Mission dwell among them. This was exciting, the launching of a beachhead into enemy territory. It was symbolized by Dr. Dick Anderson's driving a stake into the hard rocky soil, claiming the area and the people of the tribe for God.

As a result, a hospital and school were built. Dr. Dick and Joan Anderson served together with their colleagues, Paul and Betty Teasdale and Rev. and Mrs. Peter Mualuku, a dedicated Kenyan couple who eventually served in that tribe for a period of 25 years. Today,

Dr. "Dick" Anderson staking claim at Lokori.

12 stations have been opened in this vast area that was once declared a closed district. Thus, the Lord revealed that He is able to make a way when there is no way.

Claim staking has been an integral part of our missionaries' and evangelists' ministry throughout the history of the Mission. Peter Cameron Scott, the founder of the Mission, and the early pioneers were God's claimstakers. His goal was to plant stations from the port of Mombasa, Kenya, all the way up to Chad in central Africa, but he never saw the fulfillment of his vision as he succumbed to the disease of malaria. However, even on his deathbed, his heart concern was for the multitudes who were still in spiritual darkness, and he quoted from Psalm 107:1-3, "O give thanks unto the Lord, for He is good: for His mercy endureth forever. Let the redeemed of the Lord say so, whom He hath redeemed from the hand of the enemy; And gathered them out of the lands, from the east, from the west, from the north, and from the south."

Charles Hurlburt, the chairman of the first American Council, was stirred by the dedication and devotion of Scott. He felt constrained to take up the torch Scott had been called upon to lay down. He was also a man of vision. He and his colleagues staked claims for God in Tanganyika, Congo, Uganda, and French Equatorial Africa. A vibrant church exists in these areas, the result of the prayers and godly determination of these men and women. This church has a trained national leadership that is ministering to two million baptized believers in approximately five thousand churches.

Each of these countries show evidence of the miracle-working power of God. He opens doors that no man can shut. Such was the case in the Congo. On several occasions the mission sought to obtain permission to enter the eastern area, but was hindered by the opposition of another group within the country. Again, God opened the door. When Charles Hurlburt, the General Director, was on a short furlough in 1908, he was called to the White House by President Theodore Roosevelt. The President sought his advice concerning a hunting trip he was planning to make in East Africa. Through that contact, the President was brought in touch with the work of the A.I.M., and he was greatly impressed. President Roosevelt laid the cornerstone of Rift Valley Academy, our school for missionary children. Before leaving Africa, he

President "Teddy" Roosevelt and Charles Hurlburt.

said to Mr. Hurlburt, "If there is ever a time I can be of help to you, don't hesitate to call on me."

In view of the difficulties that the Mission was experiencing in getting into the Congo. Mr. Hurlburt felt constrained to write to President Roosevelt to see if he could be of assistance. As a result, President Roosevelt contacted King Albert of the Belgians and permission was granted. Therefore, in 1912, Mr. and Mrs. John Stauffacher crossed Lake Albert in a dugout canoe, climbed the slopes of the mountain, drove the stakes into the land of the Congo, and laid the groundwork for our first station at Kasengu. This led to the opening of 23 stations with more than two thousand local congregations and approximately one hundred twenty thousand baptized believers. They were led by a leadership trained in five Bible schools and Bunia Seminary. All this is evidence of God's faithfulness.

On the 80th Anniversary of the A.I.M. in 1975, the International Council of the Mission met together in London. We rejoiced in all that God had done in the past and in what He was presently doing. Then we sought to project ourselves into the future to ascertain God's plans and His future strategy. To do this, we got down on our knees. That is where claim staking really begins.

This is what the early Church did after the ascension of our risen Lord, when 120 gathered in the upper room and prayed for ten days in preparation for the final challenge given by our Lord to stake claims for God in Jerusalem, all Judea, Samaria, and in the uttermost parts of the earth. We, too, about 30 of us who were representatives of our various Home and Field Councils, also prayed earnestly, asking for the guidance of the Spirit of God. The Lord moved upon our hearts, burdening us for the unreached areas of Africa that needed to be claimed for God. Following a period of discussion, we felt constrained to launch a program of "Outreach and Advance" and we asked Dr. Dick Anderson, who was on the cutting edge of outreach in northern Kenya, to be our Secretary of Outreach. Since then, our stakes have been driven into the Seychelle Islands, Comoro Islands, the Island of Reunion, Madagascar, Mozambique, Lesotho, Namibia, and Chad. The stories of our entrance into each of these areas reads like an extension of the Book of Acts.

What happened on the Comoro Islands is a marvelous example of the way the Lord is working in many areas of the world. These four small islands were a challenge to Mr. Chris Fourie, one of God's claim stakers and Director of the South African Islands Mission. They are beautiful volcanic islands, often spoken of as "The Islands of the Moon" or "The Forgotten Islands," and are located approximately three hundred miles off the east coast of Africa in the Indian Ocean. They were colonized by the French since 1912, and had a population of 450 thousand (99.9% were Muslim).

Mr. Fourie decided to make a preliminary survey. In a unique way, he was brought into contact with Ali Sougou, a young man who was very aggressive. Ali knew French, English and several other languages. Ali became Mr. Fourie's guide and source of reference. He was very helpful in giving Mr. Fourie much information concerning the islands and its people. During the course of their conversation, Mr. Fourie had the opportunity to give him the gospel. Ali, being a staunch Muslim,

Hindu temple, Island of Reunion.

resented the message but decided to endure it. He was being paid well for his services and, after all, he would soon be leaving.

When Mr. Fourie's visit was complete, he expressed his gratitude to Ali and gave him his address in case he wanted to write to him. Ali was relieved to see him go and he thought that was the end of that, but the Holy Spirit brought to his remembrance many of the Scripture truths Mr. Fourie told him. Ali had refused a portion of the Word of God, but now he felt he would like to read the New Testament for himself, so he wrote to Chris Fourie and requested one. It was with much delight and prayer that a *Good News to Modern Man* was sent to him.

At a later date, Ali told me that he had read the New Testament seven times and, without the help of any human instructor, the Spirit of God opened his eyes to the truth and he accepted Jesus Christ as his Lord and Savior. Ali wrote to Mr. Fourie to tell him of his decision, and he went on to say, "According to the Scriptures, when one accepts Christ, he should give evidence of his faith by being baptized in His Name." He asked Chris what he should do. On receiving this word, Mr. Fourie flew to the Comoro Islands and was warmly received by Ali. Chris wanted to be sure that Ali clearly understood the gospel, so he questioned him at length and rejoiced to know that he had really accepted Christ as his personal Savior. In view of this, he was baptized in the waters of the Indian Ocean, and it was a day of great rejoicing.

Mr. Fourie would have launched his own mission program immediately, but he questioned whether the

Comorien government would permit a South African organization to start a work in their country. He, therefore, asked the Africa Inland Mission if they would accept this challenge. Following a survey by Dr. Dick

Nairobi Mosque.

Anderson, the A.I.M. agreed to accept the responsibility. Then, by faith, we staked our claim in this remote and difficult area. Shortly after our first team of two ladies started their work of translating the Scriptures, they were interrupted by the storm clouds of political unrest and had to be evacuated because of the eruption of violence.

Three of the islands demanded immediate independence from the French and eventually declared unilateral independence. The French responded by withdrawing all their doctors, nurses, teachers, administrators, technicians, and financial help. On the day they were removing their personnel, in the providence of God, Dr. Anderson was on the island.

He felt great concern for the patients who were in the large city hospital without expatriate medical doctors. He offered his services to the new President and was accepted. He worked feverishly but couldn't keep up with the load of demands made on him. He sent an urgent request to our Kenya field for help, and two doctors and several nurses and engineers responded to run the hospital. They labored with such love and concern, beyond the call of duty, that the people said, "Never have we seen such devotion." The Lord prospered their medical and surgical skills to such an extent that their fame spread to all the other islands.

This also came to the attention of the President, and he wondered who all the medics were because he had only given permission to one doctor. He, therefore, asked them to appear in his office, and the first question he asked was, "Who are you?" Peter Brashler, the leader of the group spoke French fluently. He feared that if he said, "We are missionaries," they would be expelled. So, he quickly breathed up a prayer: "Lord, what shall I say?" And he felt that the Lord prompted him by saying, "Tell him the truth." So Peter said, "We are missionaries," but he continued "Just as Jesus (Issa), whom the Muslims believe to be a prophet, showed love and compassion for the people of His day, so we want to show the love of *Issa* to the Comorien people."

The President was astounded at his answer and said that he wanted them to speak over the national radio station to tell the populace what Christianity really was. Peter thought that it would be a one-time opportunity, but instead he was on the air every Sunday evening, prime time, for a half hour. The program and message were presented in an attractive way, using recorded African choirs, quartets, and solos with a guitar accompaniment. It became very popular. In order to curtail its popularity in a Muslim country, they were forced by the government to change the format. Questions were to be asked by an interrogator. Peter Brashler feared that this would not appeal to the audience, but it proved otherwise because the questions were answered directly from the Scriptures. Although Peter felt discouraged, nevertheless, the Word made an impact upon some who responded positively, accepting Christ as their Savior.

The medical outreach continued to establish a unique relationship with the government and the Comorien people, contributing greatly to the accomplishment of our goals. Following the initial thrust by the temporary emergency team, Dr. Bill Barnett and his wife, Laura, veteran missionaries who had served in Tanzania and Kenya, felt called of the Lord to this

Comorien thrust. The success of his work, as chief surgeon in the main hospital in the capital city of Moroni, endeared him to the people and gave prestige with the government. In spite of limited equipment, he raised the medical standards of the hospital. Patients said that they had confidence in him because he prayed before each operation. The president honored him on several occasions. Once Dr. Bill responded to a Presidential medical emergency request by cutting short his four-month furlough. Upon his arrival he was given an outstanding welcome; all government offices were closed to celebrate his return. At a later date, at the request of Dr. Bill, the government transferred the responsibility of the entire Mitsamiouli hospital to him and our A.I.M. medical team.

The goodwill of the government was stimulated by the medical outreach and opened the way for 20 others to be involved in various aspects of work, such as teachers, public health workers, translators, agriculturalists, and veterinary ministries. All these outlets were channels through which we had the opportunity to quietly share the love of Christ.

Ali Sougou was permitted to go to Kenya to pursue his education. He entered the Pwani Bible Institute in Mombasa and was a zealous student and witness for Christ. During the term break, he returned to the Comoro Islands to be with his family. Upon his arrival he was immediately arrested because they learned that he had been studying the Scriptures. He was kept in solitary confinement in a room so small that he couldn't even lie down. The food was heavily salted and hardly palatable. This was his dwelling place for three months. The officials were amazed that he lived and was in good health. At his trial they gave him three options: life imprisonment, execution by a firing squad, or deportation from the island. He said he couldn't choose any of them because his family would suffer. He told them to make the choice and then on his knees, he prayed aloud, "Lord Jesus, here am I and I know You are with me; I need Your answer to these people. Amen." The crowd, listening intently, cried out, "Let this crazy man go home." To Ali's great surprise, that was the decision. Before releasing him, they tried to force him to burn his Bible and his Bible school notes, but he refused, so the official poured kerosene on them and set them ablaze. Then the judge called the Commissioner of Police and told him to provide Ali with transportation for the 25 miles to his home.

The testimony of Ali's life and quiet witness caused many in the community to be amazed at the way he endured persecution for his faith in Christ. Some asked him questions and his answers stimulated further inquiries. Thus, the "good news" began to spread, and in spite of harassment, there were those who made professions of faith. All that took place was part of the travail that gave birth to a mighty claim staker for God.

The Lord also worked in marvelous ways, His wonders to perform, in the beautiful tropical islands of the Seychelles, which were a thousand miles out in the Indian Ocean. Their 75 thousand inhabitants stood as a challenge. Many claimed to be Christians, but showed little evidence, because they linked their Christianity with the traditions of animism.

The only way we could get into this country, which was pursuing communism, was by accepting the invitation of the Minister of Education to start a ceramics school. This was God's means of enabling us to drive our stakes into this remote area of the world. In the providence of God, one of our Kenya missionaries, Jack Wilson, had his Master's degree in ceramics and he accepted this as a call from the Lord. Veteran missionaries Stanley and Carmel Kline, from Zaire, and Brian and Kathy DeSmidt, from South Africa, were part of the first team. The government provided the building and equipment, and classes were started. Students were given not only practical instruction but also teaching about the wonderful work of the Divine Potter, who was desirous of molding their lives into beautiful vessels that He could use. Jack Wilson's prowess as an athlete earned him the privilege of coaching the national basketball team, which presented many opportunities for a witness to reach young people. After several years, the ceramics project was turned over to national leadership and now the government has asked us to be in charge of a Youth Development Program for delinquents. All this has resulted in the establishment of an evangelical church that is preparing leadership to reach their fellow countrymen for Christ.

One might ask the question, "How does a mission organization penetrate a totally communistic country like Mozambique?" After a long and bitter revolution with Russian assistance the people of Mozambique obtained their independence in 1975 after 470 years of Portuguese colonial rule and emerged as a strong Marxist state. Christians were severely persecuted, missionaries were expelled, and pastors were intimidated and imprisoned. Churches and institutions were seized or destroyed. The door of opportunity opened only when famine struck the land and more than 100 thousand died of starvation. War material from Russia did not meet this need. Food provided by the United States and western countries softened the attitude of the leadership toward the West. It was at such a time as this, in the providence of God, that Dr. Dick Anderson was granted permission to make a survey trip into the area around Beira. He made contacts with and encouraged pastors who had been suppressed. This was the beginning of driving in stakes and claiming the area for God. Churches appealed to the government to allow missionaries to come in to assist in the training of national pastors, and this was granted.

The first A.I.M. team of three entered in 1986, and today there are 25 serving in various capacities. A Bible school has been established, and there is a deep hunger for the Word of God. The churches heartily welcome the preaching of the missionaries. All this continues to take place, in the midst of civil strife, in the northern part of the country by a group called the Ronamo, who oppose the communistic leadership of the country. This has taken a great toll in lives and hundreds of thousands have sought refuge in surrounding countries. The northern province presents a great challenge as there are approximately three million of the Mukua tribe who are unreached. Hopefully, the recent peace agreement and free elections will bring peace, and missionaries will be able to enter this area.

Time would fail to tell of the claim stakers who have penetrated the urban areas of the United States—in Paterson, New Jersey; Philadelphia, Pennsylvania; Winter Garden, Florida; and Detroit, Michigan—and the large African cities such as Nairobi, the capital of Kenya, referred to as the Green City in the Sun, with lovely trees and flowers that bloom all year round. Its modern buildings and hotels appear as skyscrapers, and thousands of tourists visit there each year; but the city they see is different from the one that the masses of people exist in. However, there is an ever-growing elite among Kenyans who have good jobs and homes; but then there are still the large number who live in one of the slum areas like Kibera.

Many young adults, after finishing whatever education is available in their villages, come to their "dream city," where they hope to "make it big." Unfortunately, they are confronted with too many people seeking too few jobs. Without employment, their dreams become nightmares and they are ashamed to return to their villages as a failure. They end up in shanty towns with neither funds nor families. They construct flimsy shelters or sleep on the street. Having no light, water, or sanitation, they become targets of disease. A place such as Kibera becomes a gold mine of opportunity where claims are staked for God.

Pastor Francis Ngila started a Bible study in this area with 35 and today more than 2,000 gather together. Their small church has been replaced with one that will seat 4,000. Their ministries have been increased in evangelistic outreach. There are classes for new believers, and technical training enables them to develop skills and become productive. Job 24:12a (NIV) states, "The groans of the dying rise from the city." Those groans become a Macedonia call to God's claim stakers who have responded with the Word of God. This is making the difference in the lives of hundreds who are coming to the Lord.

Ever since the inception of the work of the Africa Inland Mission, one of our main purposes has been the training of nationals in our Bible schools, Bible colleges, and seminaries, and by way of Theological Education by Extension (TEE), to be "claim stakers" for God. As a result, today we have over five thousand churches scattered throughout the countries where we are serving. Now our great concerns are for the numerous ethnic groups scattered in remote areas that are still without a witness. The A.I.C. and A.I.M. are focusing upon these. To meet this great need, a specialized "Missionary Training College" was started in Eldoret, Kenya, in January, 1986, with 11 students. In 1991 it trained 48 church leaders from 5 African countries and 8 denominations. They are all graduates of theological colleges or seminaries, who feel called of the Lord to be "claim stakers" among tribes that are in spiritual darkness. Following in-depth cross-cultural training, they are sent out to unreached tribes to carry out a four-month practical assignment by living among and witnessing to those who are considered to be "hidden people." Their goal is to establish a church that will be a lighthouse for God among the tribe, and the Lord has blessed this outreach. The college is now packed to capacity with eager students, and many more desire to come.

In fulfillment of the burden and vision of our founder, Peter Cameron Scott, a survey team was sent to the Chad, on the invitation of other missions already laboring in the southern part of the country. They encouraged us to seek to penetrate the central area, where there are approximately two million unreached. A team of four missionaries and a Chadian pastor and his wife, led by Ben Webster, traveled 4,750 miles, visited 240 villages, and made contact with 53 tribes, 29 of which had no gospel witness. Basically, they were following the traditions of their forefathers. Some have linked this with the teaching of Islam. The team was well received wherever they went. Since then they have established two bases of operation, staking their claims to reach those who have not heard. In 1990 they entered the Kwang tribe, and in 1991 the Ndam. Churches are now being planted, but the task is gigantic and the great need is for personnel.

All that has taken place is evidence of what God has done for the A.I.M. down through the nearly one hundred years of our history. Now our concern is about staking our claims among the 12 thousand people groups throughout the world who are still waiting to hear the "good news."

Missionary strategists have written much to stimulate and mobilize the Church of Christ to action concerning its responsibility to fulfill the Lord's great commission to spread the "...good news of great joy...for all the people" (Lk. 2:10 NIV) and "...among all nations" (Lk. 24:47 NIV). This means reaching groups who do not have a viable, active church movement, but it does not exclude reaching the lost in towns and cities or in the marketplace.

We are excited about what is taking place in the A.D. 2000 Movement, which is an amalgamated effort of evangelical Christianity to band together by prayer and fellowship for the purpose of establishing "a church for every people and the gospel for every person by A.D. 2000."

Presently, one of the major goals of the A.I.C. and A.I.M. is to send teams of national pastors and missionaries to evangelize and plant churches among 20 unreached tribes by 1995, the 100th Anniversary of the Mission. These groups have already been targeted, and "claim stakers" are in the process of occupying them. Some of our experienced and new missionaries have volunteered and have been assigned to the task. However, occupying 20 "hidden people groups" is but the beginning of what needs to be done. Continued surveys reveal that there are over one hundred groups in our fields who remain unreached.

A.I.M. will endeavor to accomplish this in partnership with supporting churches by urging them to participate in an "Adopt-A-People" program. This is done by "linking" each church with an identified unreached people group. The launching of a beachhead into enemy territory demands a strong support team to back up the invading army. In the same manner, the "Adopt-A-People Partners" are an essential part of the advance and success of the teams on the front line.

The Africa Inland Mission welcomes churches or individual Christian groups who will join this thrust. Profiles of unreached people groups are made available for special prayer, and periodic updates are given concerning obstacles encountered or advances made by the claim-staking teams. Those who accept this challenge are a vital part of the action. A church in Pennsylvania accepted this challenge and their prayers resulted in the sending of two couples to be part of the team to reach the Sandawe, a tribe of 32 thousand in Tanzania; progress already is being made toward establishing the first church in that area.

Responders to the claim-staking challenge need to be aware of the words of caution uttered so long ago by Peter Cameron Scott: "It is a battle!"

A battle-worn Tanzanian pastor gives encouragement, however, as he tells of an experience he had on his first visit to see the Indian Ocean. As he stood on the sandy shoreline, he was amazed at the vast expanse of water as far as the eye could see. Then he observed the ocean swelling some distance from the land, and as it moved in closer, it rose to a towering height. Reaching its crest, it broke with a terrifying roar as it tossed itself toward him there on the shore. He was fearful that the wave would submerge him, but it stopped just a few feet from where he was standing on the beach and the scene was repeated again and again. As he pondered what was happening, he thought of what the prophet Jeremiah had said: "Fear ye not Me? saith the Lord: will ye not tremble at My presence, which have placed the sand for a bound of the sea by a perpetual decree, that it cannot pass it: and though the waves thereof toss themselves, yet can they not prevail; though they roar, yet can they not pass over it?" (Jer. 5:22)

Thank God, that He, who by His power and wisdom set the sand as a bound on the boisterous tossing waves of the sea, is the One who, in His sovereignty, has placed a bound on the trying circumstances and seeming destruction that would try to envelop the African Church, and the missionaries and cause of Christ as a whole. But, the Lord Himself, by a perpetual decree, has said, "I will build My church; and the gates of hell shall not prevail against it" (Mt. 16:18b).

I am reminded of the final words of challenge given by one of my colleagues, Austin Paul, with whom I shared many evangelistic campaigns in the bush. He was a gifted evangelist and trained many others as preachers and trumpeters. After forty years of strenuous ministry he came down with a heart ailment. While on his last furlough, the Mission doctor questioned whether he should return to the Congo. During the time he was in the United States, he had urged Jack Wyrtzen to hold an evangelistic campaign in Africa. Jack's positive response thrilled Austin and really spurred him on to make preparation to get back on the field and to arrange for the thrust that would be made in the Congo. In view of the circumstances, the Mission permitted him to return.

He worked diligently with the African Church leaders to lay the groundwork for the arrival of Jack and fellow evangelists, Charlie Dawson, an Afro-American Pastor, and Harry Bollback. However, the physical strain proved to be too strenuous for Austin's condition and necessitated his being in and out of the hospital on several occasions. Then, he went into a coma for a period of time. Ed Schuit, one of Austin's fellow missionaries was asked to assist him. When Ed visited him in the hospital, Austin had all the amplification equipment around his bedroom, ready for action. As they talked about the campaign, Austin's eyes brightened with great enthusiasm, but he was very weak and gasping for breath. Between the gasps, he spoke very falteringly and said, "We've got to—we've got to—give it—give it—all we've got." Ed said it didn't look like he had much to give it physically, but in his heart he was giving it all that "he got." It was only a short time after that he went to be with the Lord. Several months after his death, I stood by the mound of his freshly made grave. The temporary headstone was only a rock and his name was painted on it—S. Austin Paul—he'd given it all that "he'd got!"

On one occasion, while in the Pearl River office, I received an emergency phone call from Nairobi that startled me and caused me to realize that the cost of the conflict can be high when it is paid for in missionaries' lives. Harold Bowman, one of four keen young pilots, landed his plane at the Juba airport in Southern Sudan. A short time after he arrived, he learned that a skirmish had broken out between two factions in the Sudan army, and he was advised by the government not to go out to his plane because it was dangerous. Several days later he was informed that the difficulties in the army had been terminated and he could proceed to the airport. On his way out in a car, a lone dissident soldier hiding in the bush opened up his Bren gun on Harold, and Harold was ushered into the presence of the Lord.

Harold Bowman gave his all.

Harold was a young man who was totally committed to the Lord. His godly parents told me quite a bit about his background and dedication. For a period of three years he was an instructor in an aeronautical school in Ohio. When one of his former students heard of his death, he wrote to the parents, saying, "I was impressed about two things each time I entered Harold's office. The first was a large map of the world on the wall, and the other was that he had a motto on the wall which read, 'Only one life, 'twill soon be past. Only what's done for Christ will last.'" Harold Bowman was linked with God in His plan for world outreach, and like His Master, he gave his all.

Therefore, whatever the cost may be, as claim stakers for God, let us strive to run the race before us, laying hold upon His promises and "...press toward the mark for the prize of the high calling of God in Christ Jesus" (Phil. 3:14), giving it all we've got!

In all that I have written, I have endeavored to unfold the marvels of the outworking of God's providential plan for one's life. As the Scriptures say, "I will instruct thee and teach thee in the way which thou shalt go: I will guide thee with Mine eye" (Ps. 32:8). This was my experience through my early years, leading to my conversion, my commitment for service in Africa, my preparation for ministry, my call to the Africa Inland Mission, and eventually the challenges in Zaire, Sudan, and the United States A.I.M. office.

I feel somewhat like Joshua must have felt when he reminded the children of Israel about all that God had done for them through the years of their early history—from the call of Abraham and all that followed, up to their entrance into the promised land—and concluded with these words, "...that not one thing hath failed of all the good things which the Lord your God spake concerning you; all are come to pass unto you, and not one thing hath failed thereof" (Josh. 23:14b). Certainly, "This is the Lord's doing; it is marvelous in our eyes" (Ps. 118:23). Therefore, all the glory and praise is to our wonderful Lord.